DATE DUE

B27   08/01 $26.60

COUNTRIES OF THE WORLD

Iran

Gareth Stevens Publishing

A WORLD ALMANAC EDUCATION GROUP COMPANY

About the Author: Dr. Maria O'Shea is a research associate of the Geopolitics and International Boundaries Research Centre at the School of Oriental and African Studies, University of London. In addition to working on the center's current research projects, she teaches undergraduate and postgraduate classes in political geography, the geography of the Middle East, and the geography of minorities. She also works as an independent consultant and writer on the Middle East. She is the author of several books on Middle Eastern countries.

PICTURE CREDITS
Archive Photos: 16, 49, 75, 77, 78, 79, 80, 81, 82
Camera Press: 52, 76
Focus Team: 63, 91
HBL Network: Cover, 19, 34, 36, 37, 85, 87
The Hutchison Library: 2, 25, 43, 51 (bottom)
Earl Kowall: 3 (bottom), 4, 6, 17, 26, 32, 41, 42, 46, 50, 51 (top), 55, 57 (bottom), 62, 71, 73
Nazima Kowall: 3 (center), 5, 20, 21, 23, 24, 30, 33, 44, 47, 57 (top), 68, 70, 84
North Wind Picture Archives: 11
Christine Osborne: 1, 3 (top), 35, 59, 64, 66, 69
Maria O'Shea: 90 (both)
Sportestan Publishing: 72
Topham Picturepoint: 14, 15 (bottom), 56, 58, 60, 83
Trip Photographic Library: 7, 8, 9 (both), 10, 15 (top), 18, 22, 27, 28, 29, 31, 38, 39, 40, 45, 48, 53, 61, 65, 67, 74, 89
Vision Photo Agency: 12, 13, 54

Digital Scanning by Superskill Graphics Pte Ltd

Written by
MARIA O'SHEA

Edited by
KAREN KWEK

Designed by
HASNAH MOHD ESA

Picture research by
SUSAN JANE MANUEL

First published in North America in 2000 by
Gareth Stevens Publishing
A World Almanac Education Group Company
1555 North RiverCenter Drive, Suite 201
Milwaukee, Wisconsin 53212 USA

For a free color catalog describing
Gareth Stevens' list of high-quality books
and multimedia programs, call
1-800-542-2595 (USA) or
1-800-461-9120 (CANADA).
Gareth Stevens Publishing's
Fax: (414) 225-0377.

© **TIMES MEDIA PRIVATE LIMITED 2000**
Originated and designed by
Times Editions
An imprint of Times Media Private Limited
A member of the Times Publishing Group
Times Centre, 1 New Industrial Road
Singapore 536196
http://www.timesone.com.sg/te

Library of Congress Cataloging-in-Publication Data
O'Shea, Maria.
Iran / by Maria O'Shea.
p.   cm. -- (Countries of the world)
Includes bibliographical references (p. 94) and index.
Summary: An introduction to the geography, history, government, lifestyles, culture, and current issues of Iran.
ISBN 0-8368-2325-7 (lib. bdg.)
[1. Iran. 2. Iran.] I. Title. II. Countries of the world (Milwaukee, Wis.)
DS254.75.O84   2000
955--dc21   00-020832

Printed in Malaysia

1 2 3 4 5 6 7 8 9 04 03 02 01 00

Contents

AN OVERVIEW OF IRAN

Located at the crossroads of Asia and Europe, Iran is a young nation with an ancient history — modern Iran was once the heart of the mighty Persian Empire (559–330 B.C.). After the fall of the empire, Persian cultural achievements continued under Greek, Arab, and Mongol rule. It was not until the sixteenth century that Persian rulers regained power. The Islamic Republic of Iran was declared after the Islamic Revolution of 1978–1979.

Today, Iran is a melting pot of cultures. Despite losing much of its once vast empire and enduring a tumultuous past that includes foreign conquest, domestic revolution, civil strife, and war with neighboring Iraq, present-day Iran retains a strong political presence in the Middle East.

Opposite: **Some Iranian villages date back to between the second and seventh centuries.**

Below: **Residents of Esfahan, in central Iran, enjoy a walk in Esfahan Square.**

THE FLAG OF IRAN

The Iranian flag consists of horizontal green, white, and red bands. The color green stands for the Islamic faith, white for peace, and red for the Iranian people's readiness to shed blood for their country. At the top and bottom edges of the white band are the words *Allah-o-Akhbar* (AWL-lah-oo-AKH-bar), Persian for "God is great." In the center of the flag is Iran's national symbol, which is based on the word *Allah*, or "God," in calligraphic script. The current Iranian flag was adopted in 1979. It replaced the pre-revolutionary flag, which bore the lion symbol of the Pahlavi dynasty (1925–1979).

Geography

A Rugged Land

Covering an area of 636,296 square miles (1,648,000 square kilometers), Iran is more than twice the size of the state of Texas. In terms of altitude, it is one of the highest countries in the world. Except for its narrow coastal strips, Iran lies on a plateau with an average elevation of about 4,000 feet (1,219 meters).

Much of central and eastern Iran consists of vast, flat deserts of rock, sand, and salt. Villages are scattered around the deserts and throughout the mountain chains. Traditionally built of mud, these settlements are located close to water sources and usually surrounded by greenery, forming a welcome respite from the harsh desert scenery.

Mountains and Volcanoes

Three mountain ranges cut across the Iranian plateau. The Zagros Mountains in the west and southwest divide Iran from the Mesopotamian plain of Iraq. The Markazi range extends from

EARTHQUAKES

Three main fault lines, or fractures in Earth's crust, run across Iran, making it prone to earthquakes and other types of volcanic activity. Cities such as Tabriz, in the province of East Azerbaijan, have been destroyed several times over by earthquakes. In 1978, an earthquake in Tabas, in eastern Iran, killed 25,000 people. In 1990, an earthquake hit the province of Gilan, near the Caspian Sea, killing 40,000 people and leaving many more injured and homeless.

northwestern Iraq to the southeastern coast. The Elburz
Mountains in northern Iran consist of several volcanic peaks,
including Mount Damavand, which is Iran's highest peak at
18,606 feet (5,671 m).

Lakes and Plains

North of the Elburz Mountains, the land slopes down to the
Caspian Sea, which is not really a sea but the largest lake in the
world. The Caspian Sea is almost the size of Spain and half as big
as all the Great Lakes of North America put together. In southern
Iran, the Zagros Mountains descend to a barren, low-lying plain
along the Persian Gulf. The hottest part of this area is the plain of
Khuzestan, where summer temperatures can reach 124° Fahrenheit
(51° Celsius). The Karun, Iran's only navigable river, flows across
the Khuzestan plain. Most of Iran's oil fields are also located in
Khuzestan. Although dam projects have created several artificial
lakes, Iran has only one large natural body of water, Lake Urmiah,
in the northwest.

Above: **Flamingos
inhabit the coastal
regions of Iran near
the Persian Gulf.**

Opposite:
**The snowcapped
Zagros Mountains lie
beyond the plains of
central Iran.**

A Range of Climates

Northwestern and western Iran experience four seasons, with freezing winters. During the cold season, temperatures can plunge to a low of -35° F (-37° C) in the northwestern provinces of East and West Azerbaijan. Spring is greeted with delight. As the snow on the mountains melts, rushing streams and waterfalls are formed, and flowers carpet the mountain slopes.

Moving southward and eastward into Iran, the seasons of spring and autumn become shorter, merging into just two distinct seasons — summer and winter. In central, southern, and eastern Iran, the sun beats down relentlessly from April to November. The so-called "120-Day Wind" blows toward Pakistan over most of Iran. Summer changes rapidly into a mild winter, bringing rain.

The Iranian plateau receives only 2–10 inches (51–254 millimeters) of annual rainfall. The Elburz Mountains, however, trap humidity in the Caspian Sea region, giving the coastal provinces of Gilan and Mazandaran up to 79 inches (2,007 mm) of annual rainfall. The climate there is semitropical, supporting luxuriant forests, as well as rice and tea plantations.

Above: **In the hottest parts of Iran, houses have tall wind towers with openings angled to catch the breeze. Wind is directed down into the basement, where a pond or stream cools the air, which then circulates through the whole house.**

QANATS: AN ANCIENT TECHNOLOGY

Iranians have learned to live in their arid land by developing a complex system of irrigation.
(A Closer Look, page 64)

A Variety of Habitats

Apart from the areas close to the Caspian Sea, Iran has relatively little vegetation, due to the country's high altitude and harsh climate. The most common tree is the slender poplar, which grows along the banks of streams and in gardens and farms, offering precious shade from the hot summer sun. Shrubs, wild flowers, and fruit and nut trees also grow in Iran.

Most of Iran's forests are concentrated in the Caspian region, where oak, beech, elm, and ash trees grow. The Zagros Mountains support oak forests, while acacia and Jerusalem thorn trees dot the drier areas.

Because much of the land is uncultivated and uninhabited, many wild animals thrive in Iran. Forbidding mountain lairs are home to bears, lynxes, leopards, jackals, hyenas, and wolves. Gazelles and ibex also roam the highlands. Cheetahs, tigers, wild boar, gazelles, songbirds, and seals live in the fertile Caspian region. Buzzards circle the deserts, which are also home to fascinating reptiles and insects.

Iran's most common animals are camels and the sheep and goats kept for wool, dairy products, and meat. The country has more sheep and goats than people. Iranian sheep belong to a particular Middle Eastern breed. They have relatively thin bodies but store their fat in their large tails, an adaptation that enables them to survive the hot, dry conditions of Iran.

THE DELECTABLE POMEGRANATE

The pomegranate has a special place in Iran. Iranian pomegranates are possibly the reddest and most succulent in the world. Poets use the fruit and its flower to describe rubies, blood, fire, youth, and beauty. All parts of the pomegranate tree are put to good use in Iran for food, dye, or medicine. Pomegranate molasses is the basis of many Iranian dishes.

Left: The rare pygmy gecko (*Tropiocolotes latifi*) is among the many reptile species that live in the deserts of central Iran.

History

Archaeological finds point to human activity in the Zagros Mountains as far back as 100,000 B.C. By about 6000 B.C., farms and permanent settlements were widespread throughout the Iranian plateau and on the plains of present-day Khuzestan.

By about 2500 B.C., the Elamite civilization, a group that settled on the Khuzestan plains and nearby highlands to the north and east, had established a feudal system of government. About five hundred years later, isolated groups of Aryans, a fair-skinned, Indo-European people, moved into the land from regions north of the Caspian Sea.

The Elamite civilization lasted until the sixth century B.C. By that time, two groups of Aryans dominated the land — the Medes in northwestern Iran, and the Parsua, later known as *Persians*, in the southwestern regions.

The Rise and Fall of the Persian Empire

In the mid-sixth century B.C., Cyrus II, the king of the Persians, defeated the Medes. Cyrus the Great, as he was called, later conquered most of the then civilized world, creating an empire that stretched from Central Asia to the borders of Egypt.

PERSIA OR IRAN?

The name *Iran* is derived from *Aryan.* Although Iranians have always referred to their country as Iran, the rest of the world knew it as Persia until about the 1950s.

Left: **The tomb of Cyrus the Great stands in Pasargadae, in southwestern Iran. Cyrus made Pasargadae his capital because it lay near the site of his victory over the Medes.**

After Cyrus's death, his son Cambyses added Egypt to the empire. Darius the Great expanded the kingdom eastward to northern India and westward into Ionian Greek lands. Xerxes, son of Darius, continued his father's strong rule, but the kingdom declined because of later rulers' weaknesses and growing aggression from the Greek Empire. In 330 B.C., Greek ruler Alexander the Great conquered the Persian stronghold of Persepolis, burning down the royal palace.

The Persians regained their independence after Alexander's death in 323 B.C. Several dynasties ruled, including the Seleucids in Syria and Babylonia (in present-day Iraq), the Parthians in Parthia (southeast of the Elburz Mountains), and the Sasanids, successors to the Parthians. In A.D. 651, the Sasanian kingdom, weakened by clashes with the Turks and the Byzantine Empire (the eastern half of the Roman Empire), fell to the Arabs. Despite occasional Persian uprisings, the Arabs ruled until the thirteenth century, when the Mongols, led by Genghis Khan, invaded Persia from the east, destroying much of Persian and Arab civilization. To the west, the Turkish Ottoman Empire grew in strength, becoming Persia's main rival from the 1200s onward.

Above: **The Greek (*right*) and Persian armies clashed in the Battle of Plataea in 479 B.C. Alexander the Great so admired the Persian military that, in preparation for his campaign in India, he trained his troops in the skills and tactics of the Persian light cavalry.**

PERSIAN ACHIEVEMENTS

Many great Arab thinkers were, in fact, Persian. Renowned physician, scientist, and writer Avicenna, or Ibn Sina, and famous mathematician and poet Omar Khayyam lived during the period of Arab rule over Persia and wrote most of their works in Arabic.

From the Safavids to the Qajars

It was not until the sixteenth century that Persia again had a leader who could reunite its kingdoms and recapture some of its former glory. Persian Shah Abbas I (the Great) of the Safavid dynasty, which gained power in the early sixteenth century, ruled from 1588 to 1629. Persia prospered during his reign, but his less able successors suffered the ravaging of the western part of the country by the Ottoman Turks.

By the start of the twentieth century, Persia had diminished to about its present size, having lost present-day Afghanistan in the eighteenth century and the Caucasus in the north to Russia in the early nineteenth century. Clashes with Afghan forces in eastern Persia also weakened the empire. European powers, in particular Russia and Britain, posed a further threat. Oil was discovered in Khuzestan in the early 1900s and exploited by the British, who paid the Persian government only a token portion of the profits. The later Qajar rulers sold European powers many concessions for developing Persia's resources but squandered the income on luxuries.

The World Wars

World War I saw the increase of European influence in the Persian government. In 1921, disgusted by government corruption and Iran's lack of real independence, young army officer Reza Khan seized control of the armed forces in a coup, becoming minister of war. In 1925, he became Reza Shah Pahlavi, sovereign ruler of the country. The Iranians regarded him as a dictator. His far-reaching reforms were greeted with hostility by many groups, including Muslim religious leaders who felt that he was undermining Islamic traditions in Persia.

During World War II, Iran was occupied by British and Russian forces. Reza Shah Pahlavi abdicated and was succeeded by his son, Muhammad Reza Shah Pahlavi. The new ruler's attempts to nationalize the oil industry in the 1950s failed because the Western oil companies operating in Iran were determined to keep their control over the country's oil wealth.

The White Revolution

Despite opposition from some groups, Muhammad Reza Shah Pahlavi implemented sweeping reforms that became known as the "White Revolution." These changes included land redistribution

Above: **Shah Abbas the Great ruled from 1588 to 1629. He strengthened the Safavid dynasty and consolidated its authority over Persian territories by pushing back foreign invaders. He was a wise and tolerant ruler, as well as a great diplomat, warrior, administrator, builder, and patron of the arts and sciences.**

ESFAHAN: HALF THE WORLD

In the sixteenth century, Shah Abbas the Great established Esfahan as his capital and one of the most magnificent cities in the world.

(A Closer Look, page 50)

and the easing of restrictions placed on women. As Iran enjoyed prosperity during the world oil boom in 1974, however, the social and economic gap between rich and poor, modern and traditional, and urban and rural Iranians continued to widen. Corruption became widespread, and development projects were increasingly expensive and inappropriate. By 1978, groups of students, intellectuals, and religious leaders were strongly opposed to the shah's dictatorial rule.

Left: **Muhammad Reza Shah Pahlavi walks in procession through the courtyard of Golestan Palace in Tehran after his coronation in 1967. Although he had come to the throne in 1941, the shah had deferred his coronation for twenty-six years, until he could bring relative stability and progress to Iran.**

The 1978–1979 Revolution

Political discontent led to the 1978–1979 Revolution, a popular uprising against the shah's government. When the shah's hated secret service, SAVAK, wiped out all political organizations, the revolutionaries rallied together in another institution — the mosque. While many intellectuals and students wanted greater political freedom, devout Shi'ite Muslims argued that the shah's policies threatened traditional Islamic values. Gradually, religious groups became the dominant revolutionary force. Rebel leader Ruhollah (Ayatollah) Khomeini demanded the shah's abdication, and, on January 16, 1979, Muhammad Reza Shah Pahlavi fled Iran.

Khomeini became the country's leader and established the new Islamic Republic of Iran on April 1. After the revolution, many Iranians who opposed Khomeini's government were persecuted, tortured, executed, or killed by Khomeini's forces. Khomeini died of a heart attack on June 3, 1989, and was succeeded by Ayatollah Ali Khamenei as Iran's spiritual leader. Hojjatoleslam Ali Akbar Hashemi Rafsanjani was elected head of state.

The current Iranian government, headed by President Muhammad Khatami, has weathered many crises and liberalized its approach to leadership. Khatami has consistently worked toward improving relations with the West.

A SPIRITUAL LEADER

The title *Ayatollah* (EYE-ah-tol-ah), or "sign of God," is given to a Shi'ite leader who has achieved the highest level of religious learning. Other Muslims look to him as a spiritual model.

THE IRAN-IRAQ WAR

On September 22, 1980, Iraqi forces moved east across the border into western Iran, beginning a war that would last ten years and claim the lives of about one million civilian and military personnel on both sides.

(*A Closer Look,* page 54)

Cyrus the Great (c. 590/580–529 B.C.)

Cyrus II, or Cyrus the Great, was a mighty ruler and a capable and humane administrator. He expanded the Persian Empire westward, from Medes to the Ionian Greek kingdoms of the Aegean Sea, to Babylonia (including present-day Syria and Israel). Cyrus established several capitals, including Ecbatana (present-day Hamadan) and Pasargadae, in Persis (present-day Fars).

Muhammad Reza Shah Pahlavi (1919–1980)

The eldest son of Reza Shah Pahlavi, Muhammad Reza Shah Pahlavi became shah of Iran in 1941. He called himself the Imperial Majesty, King of Kings of the Aryans, and traced his ancestry to Cyrus the Great. In 1963, he launched the White Revolution, which redistributed land from the big landowners to the peasants and provided free education, social welfare, and health care. The shah also introduced many laws to give women more freedom. However, his opponents charged that he squandered much of Iran's vast oil wealth on a lavish lifestyle. His autocratic rule alienated the people. Nobody was allowed to criticize him or his policies, and all Iranian intellectuals lived in fear of his secret police. The revolution of 1978–1979 forced the shah to leave Iran. He died soon afterward in exile in Egypt.

Muhammad Reza Shah Pahlavi

Ruhollah Khomeini (c. 1900–1989)

As a Shi'ite scholar and teacher, Ruhollah Khomeini took a stand against the Iranian ruler Muhammad Reza Shah Pahlavi in the 1960s. By that time, Khomeini held the title of Grand Ayatollah and commanded the support of many Iranians. Exiled for his antigovernment activities in 1964, he lived first in Iraq and then in Paris. From there, in the 1970s, his tape-recorded messages arrived in Iran, inciting Iranians against the shah and forcing the shah's abdication in 1979. Khomeini returned to Iran from France and was made the political and religious leader of Iran for life. His rule marked a departure from the pro-Western policies of the leaders before him and a return to strict Islamic values. Despite a floundering economy and the trials of the Iran-Iraq War, Khomeini received widespread Iranian support until his death.

Ruhollah Khomeini

Government and the Economy

An Islamic Government

The 1978–1979 Revolution established the current system of Islamic government. The *faqih* (fah-KEEH), or supreme spiritual leader, has final authority in all government matters and ensures that the country is ruled in accordance with Islamic laws. The current faqih is Ayatollah Ali Khamenei.

The head of state is the president, who is popularly elected every four years and must be a Muslim male. The president appoints a cabinet of twenty-four ministers. An elected parliament of 270 members, called the *Majlis* (MAJ-liss), or the Islamic Consultative Assembly, approves laws and makes economic decisions. The Council of Guardians, a panel of Islamic judges and scholars, supervises elections and ensures that the laws passed by the Majlis conform to Islamic beliefs and values. Six of the council's twelve members are appointed by the faqih. The remaining six are nominated by the High Council of the Judiciary.

Above: **Iran's current president, Muhammad Khatami, was elected in 1997.**

The Law and the Judiciary

The Qur'an, the Islamic holy book, offers detailed laws and regulations concerning almost all aspects of life, as well as punishments for breaking those laws. Additional advice and instructions are found in the Hadith (the collected sayings and teachings of the Prophet Muhammad) and in the writings of the great Islamic scholars and teachers.

Two branches of Iranian law are unique to Islam. *Hodood* (hoh-DOOD) offences include adultery, drinking alcohol, and theft, and punishments for these are all clearly described in Islamic law. *Qessas* (gheh-SAAS) are crimes punishable by retribution. Murder, for example, earns the death penalty. Personal injury is dealt with according to similar principles of retribution.

The Iranian legal system has been based on Islamic law since 1979, with the clergy acting as judges. There are several levels of courts, ranging from civil courts to the Supreme Court. Judges operate without juries. Revolutionary Courts function separately, dealing mostly with political and national security matters.

Administration

Iran is currently divided into twenty-eight provinces. New ones are created as the population increases. Each province, or *ostan* (oos-TAAN), is administered by a governor-general, or *ostandar* (oos-TAAN-dar), who is based in the provincial capital. Every town, or *shahr* (SHAR), is administered by a *farmandar* (far-man-DAR), and every village by a *kadkhoda* (kad-KHOD-a). Each city elects a mayor, or *shahrdar* (shar-DAR).

The Armed Forces

In addition to its permanent and noncommissioned officers, the Iranian national army is made up of male conscripts, aged eighteen and above, who serve for two years. No women are permitted to serve in the regular army. Iran has another army called the Pasdaran, or the Islamic Revolutionary Guard Corps. Founded in 1979, this army is responsible for guarding politicians and government centers and for enforcing Islamic revolutionary values. The Pasdaran has women's divisions.

MILITARY STATISTICS

In 1999, the Iranian army numbered 350,000, the navy 18,000, and the air force 30,000. There are 350,000 possible reserve forces and 120,000 Revolutionary Guards. Defense spending for the 1998–1999 Iranian fiscal year was U.S. $5.8 billion, or 2.9 percent of Iran's gross domestic product.

Below: **Tehran is the capital of Iran. The Elburz Mountains form a dramatic backdrop to the city skyline.**

The Economy

In the 1990s, the Iranian government announced plans to diversify its oil-reliant economy. Nevertheless, several factors have contributed to slow economic growth during this period. The Iran-Iraq War, which lasted throughout the 1980s, left the country with U.S. $1 trillion in damages. Although the strong oil market of 1996 helped Iran pay off some of its national debt, oil prices hit a record low in 1998 and early 1999. Industrial investment plunged by 40 percent as many factories across Iran closed down. Despite successful attempts to forge new trading partnerships, Iran's economy has been badly damaged since the mid-1990s by U.S. trade sanctions. In 1999, Iran faced an inflation rate of 14.2 percent and an unemployment rate of about 20 percent.

THE BAZAARS OF IRAN

When you enter an Iranian *bazaar* (bah-ZAHR), you step into a bustling, bewildering world of trade and commerce.
(A Closer Look, page 46)

IMPORTS AND EXPORTS

Machinery, military supplies, food, and pharmaceuticals are among Iran's imports. Major exports are oil, oil products, and natural gas. Iran also exports handmade carpets, fruits, nuts, leather, and caviar. The country's main trading partners are Japan, Western Europe, and Turkey.

Left: A fisherman carries his crates and fishing net. Northern Iran prospers from its caviar industry. Fishing, forestry, and agriculture contribute a significant part of Iran's gross national product.

Natural Resources and Industry

Although some experts argue that Iran's large and young population is its greatest potential resource, Iran's most valuable natural resource is oil. The country also has deposits of iron and copper, and its vast natural gas fields supply most of its cities with gas for domestic and industrial use. Pipelines also carry gas to Iran's northern neighbors and Turkey.

About one-fifth of the Iranian labor force works in the industrial sector. The biggest industries in Iran are involved in extracting, refining, and creating products from oil. Most refineries are based in southern Iran, close to the oilfields. Iran's steel industry centers around the city of Esfahan. Large industries throughout Iran include mining and automobile, textile, and carpet manufacturing.

OIL: "BLACK GOLD"

Iran's fortunes have been built on oil, but what will happen when its oil fields run dry?
(*A Closer Look, page 60*)

Despite the hardships of farming in Iran and the fact that less than half of the land is suitable for growing crops, more than one-third of Iranians work in agricultural jobs. Wheat and barley are the country's most important crops. Other crops include cotton, fruits, rice, sugar beets, potatoes, nuts, tea, tobacco, saffron, and henna. The Caspian area supports thriving silk and caviar industries, and Iranian pistachio nuts are reputedly the best in the world.

Above: **An Iranian employed in a factory inspects shelves of canned food.**

People and Lifestyle

A Multicultural Nation

Most modern Iranians are descended from the Aryan groups who came from Central Asia in the second millennium B.C. The Persians, whose mother tongue is Persian, or Farsi, represent only a slight majority in Iran. Just under half of all Iranians belong to other distinct ethnic or linguistic groups, including the Azerbaijanis, Kurds, Arabs, Baluchis, and Lurs. Although they may speak and write Farsi, they have distinct languages and cultures.

Up to 25 percent of Iranians speak Turkic languages. The largest Turkic-speaking group is the Azerbaijanis, a people who occupy northwestern Iran and the neighboring Republic of Azerbaijan. Like other Iranians, Azerbaijanis are Shi'ite Muslims. They play an active part in the social, economic, cultural, and political life of the country. Other Turkic speakers include the Qashqai, concentrated north of the Persian Gulf, and the Turkmen, who possess the Asiatic features of their Mongol ancestors and live in northeastern Iran.

NOMADIC PEOPLES

Groups such as the Bakhtiari and the Qashqai have been practicing their wandering lifestyle for hundreds of years. Now, due to modernization and government pressure, more and more nomadic groups are setting up permanent settlements.
(*A Closer Look, page 56*)

Below: Modern Iranians trace their ancestry back some four thousand years.

The Kurds live in Iran's western mountains and across the border in Iraq and Turkey. Most are Sunni Muslims. Many Kurds want their own nation and have struggled against governments in Iraq and Turkey as well as in Iran.

The Rural-Urban Divide

Although Iranians come from varied ethnic and religious backgrounds, perhaps the widest national divide exists between urban and rural dwellers. Agriculture remains a major economic sector, but more and more people are leaving their villages and farms in search of better employment, education, and health-care opportunities in the cities.

An additional gulf separates the capital, Tehran, from other provincial cities. Because Tehran is far ahead in terms of services and infrastructure, Iranians all across Iran are attracted to the capital and the modern lifestyle it offers. About 60 percent of Iranians now live in cities, with more than one-sixth of the entire population crowded into Tehran.

MINORITIES

Most of Iran's minority peoples, including Kurds, Lurs (*above*), Arabs, and Baluchis, live close to the borders. The Iranian government works hard at encouraging these groups to feel a sense of belonging in Iran, regardless of their ethnic origins.

Family Life

Almost all life in Iran revolves around the family. Most Iranians are very close to their family members, relying on them for support through life's emotional or financial troubles. Many Iranians live in multigenerational households, in which the grandparents help to care for children and are in turn cared for in old age. Although young Iranians may leave home to set up independent households, most still prefer to live close to their parents. Very few Iranians live alone, and almost everyone sees a good marriage as essential in life. Families expect to have close relationships with their in-laws. Marriage is seen not as the loss of a family member but as a chance to expand the family.

Today, due to changing lifestyles and a growing recognition of the importance of providing education for children, Iranian families tend to be smaller than in the past. Children are included in most social occasions. To be a relative is to belong, and family members, even distant relatives, eat together regularly, often without any invitation or advance notice.

Above: **At an oasis near the ancient city of Bam, a family enjoys a picnic in the shade of date palms. Picnics are a popular family activity in Iran.**

Social Roles

Islamic and social conventions make the eldest male the head of the family, but this has not diminished the strong character of many Iranian women. Wisdom is thought to come with the experience of age, and the elderly are generally well respected in Iranian society.

Marriage

Under Islamic law, an Iranian man is permitted to have up to four wives, a custom still practiced among some religious and rural groups. Most Iranian men, however, rarely have more than one wife.

Once weaned, Iranian children are considered the property of the father and his family. In the event of divorce or the mother's death, the children usually live with their father or his parents.

GETTING MARRIED IN IRAN

Traditional Zoroastrian customs and symbolic gifts make an Iranian wedding an especially memorable occasion.
(A Closer Look, page 52)

Below: **An Iranian family relaxes in the gardens of Golestan Palace in Tehran.**

Education

About 75 percent of Iranians above the age of fifteen can read and write, although this figure is much lower in rural areas and among women. Elementary and secondary education is free and compulsory from the ages of six to fourteen. Iranians highly value education, and university degrees are especially sought after. Only financial constraints and the high academic standards prevent most school leavers from completing their education or pursuing higher education.

Graduating high school students must take both national and local examinations for admittance to universities. The students' choices of courses and universities are determined by their high school examination results. Iranians generally regard medicine as the most prestigious and difficult course, and many consider Tehran universities, followed by other major provincial universities, the most desirable institutions of higher learning.

Competition to enter universities is fierce. Because some places are reserved for the heroes of the Iran-Iraq War and their families, the remaining places are difficult to secure. Aside from their academic qualifications, candidates must be of good

A TOUGH SYSTEM

The Iranian education system focuses on discipline and on memorizing set texts. Arabic, English, and Qur'an studies are compulsory. If a student fails any subject in the summer examinations, he or she has to retake the exam at the end of the summer. A second failure in even one subject means repeating the entire year. After the first eleven years of general education, students specialize in a more focused group of subjects, such as the natural sciences or the humanities.

character, knowledgeable about Islam, and not involved in illegal activities. Most students spend up to a year preparing for the university entrance exams and may take several exams in one summer. Those who can afford private tutors usually have a greater chance of success.

More than one million Iranians are currently attending institutions of higher learning. Half of these students are enrolled at private, fee-paying institutions. To repay their tuitions at state institutions, the government requires graduates in certain fields to work in remote areas of Iran for a period of time after graduation.

Religious and Adult Education

There are several other types of education in Iran. Many children attend Friday Qur'an classes taught by a local *mullah* (MOOL-ah), or religious expert. Some boys and young men attend religious schools, after which they continue their training to become mullahs at religious seminaries in cities such as Qom. The government promotes an active program of adult education, and adult literacy classes are held in the evenings.

Opposite: **Schoolboys play in a park in Tehran.**

Below: **Schoolgirls enjoy a break between classes. In Iranian schools, boys and girls are taught separately from an early age, boys by men and girls by women. At universities, some classes are mixed, but men and women sit on opposite sides of the classroom.**

Shi'ite and Sunni Islam

Ninety-nine percent of Iranians are Muslims — 89 percent belong to the Shi'ite branch, and 10 percent are Sunnis. All Muslims believe in one God, Allah, and that Muhammad was His last prophet. Differences between Shi'ites and Sunnis first arose after the death of Prophet Muhammad and are still, sometimes, sorely felt today. While Shi'ite Muslims recognize only Muhammad's descendants as legitimate leaders of the Islamic world, Sunnis accept other claims to leadership. While Shi'ite Muslims live in Iran and other Middle Eastern countries, Sunnis predominate among the Arabs, Turks, and Pakistanis.

More Than a Place of Prayer

Shi'ite rulers are political as well as religious leaders. The mosque is not only a place to pray; it is also a communal meeting place. Friday sermons can be an opportunity to learn about politics as well as faith. Mosques were the rallying places for supporters of Khomeini and the Islamic Revolution of 1978–1979. During the 1970s, mosques distributed money, information, and instructions to the revolutionaries.

Below: **Iranian women stream out of a mosque in Esfahan after Friday prayers.**

Other Faiths

Non-Muslims make up only about 1 percent of Iranians. They are generally free to practice their religion, as long as they respect Islam. About 200,000 Christians, mainly Orthodox Armenians, live in Iran. Many of Iran's 25,000 Jews live in Tehran. The 100,000 or so Zoroastrians are concentrated in Tehran and in central and southeastern Iran. These minorities are represented by allocated seats in the Majlis.

The Iranian government has arrested and persecuted followers of the Baha'i faith, which Muslim authorities consider anti-Islamic. Baha'is believe that all the founders of the major world religions are manifestations, or forms, of the same God. Today, Baha'is number between 300,000 and 350,000 in Iran.

The Evil Eye

Iranians are fond of charms and amulets. Many Iranian children wear blue beads or jewelry with turquoise stones. These allegedly guard against the "evil eye," a curse thought to be cast when someone looks jealously at another's possessions or envies another's good fortune. Anything precious is, therefore, often protected with a charm. Common Iranian amulets include images of small golden hands, pictures of the Shi'ite leader Ali, seashells, and Qur'an verses written on metal charms or on paper and encased in decorative containers.

ZOROASTRIANISM
According to most historical sources, Zoroastrianism began in Iran in the sixth century B.C. Some Zoroastrians, however, believe that their faith is hundreds of years older. This ancient religion still has followers in modern Iran.
(A Closer Look, page 70)

Language and Literature

The official language of Iran is Persian, also known as Farsi. Only about half of all Iranians, however, speak Farsi as a first language. Native speakers of Turkic languages and dialects make up about one-fourth of the population. About 9 percent speak Kurdish. Other languages spoken in Iran include Luri, Baluchi, Arabic, and numerous minority languages and dialects.

An Indo-European language, Farsi shares roots with most European languages, such as English, German, French, and Spanish. Farsi, or modern Persian, is derived from two older forms of Persian — Old Persian, spoken before 200 B.C., and Middle Persian, spoken between 200 B.C. and A.D. 1000. Modern Persian is written in Arabic characters. Many English words come from Farsi, including *khaki*, *paradise*, *pajamas*, and *lozenge.*

Literature

Iranian achievements in literature are well established. Famous Iranian poets include Ferdowsi, who lived in the tenth and eleventh centuries and wrote the *Shahnamah*, or *Book of Kings*, an

Left: **Iran is a nation of avid readers.**

THE PERSIAN NIGHTS?

The *Arabian Nights*, or *Tales of 1001 Nights*, was originally a collection of Persian stories written in Arabic.

SHIRAZ

The city of Shiraz, in the province of Fars, is renowned for the tombs of poets Hafez and Saadi. Hafez's marble tombstone, inscribed with his verses, lies inside a small pavilion (*left*) built in 1953. The mausoleum grounds include a teahouse set around a rectangular pool. The tomb of Saadi stands in a picturesque garden. The current monument was built in 1952, replacing an earlier, simpler structure.

epic about Iran's history before the Arab invasion. Perhaps the most well-known Iranian poet outside Iran is Omar Khayyam, whose eleventh-century work the *Rubaiyat* has been translated into many languages, including English. Saadi, a thirteenth-century Iranian poet, wrote *Bustan* (*The Orchard*) and *Golestan* (*The Rose Garden*), famous moral tales penned in a mixture of prose and verse. The fourteenth-century Iranian poet Hafez is best admired for his splendid *ghazals*, or lyric poems. Iran's contemporary poets hold an important position in Iranian society.

After poetry, short stories are the most common form of Iranian fiction. Novels have been written since the 1950s. Famous novelists and short story writers include Simin Daneshvar and her late husband, Jalal Al-e Ahmad, and Sadeq Hedayat, author of *The Blind Owl*, which was critically acclaimed both in Iran and internationally. Iranian writer Mahmoud Doulatabadi published the first multi-volume Iranian novel, *Kelidar*, in 1985.

In Iran, literature is more than just entertainment. Many writers and intellectuals use their work to educate the public, examining and exposing negative aspects of Iranian society and politics. As a result, many Iranian writers have been persecuted by the authorities and have had their works banned. Since 1979, all publications, including magazines and newspapers, are subject to government approval. Writers can be punished for producing works that the state deems unacceptable.

TRADITIONAL ENTERTAINMENT

Much as they have done for centuries, traveling storytellers still entertain audiences in traditional Iranian villages. In front of a painted backdrop that forms a setting for the tales, the storyteller narrates the exploits of ancient heroes and the lives of religious figures. The stories, often recited in verse, may unfold in several installments over a few days. The villagers feed, house, and offer money to the storyteller to hear more. Traditional storytellers also entertain in teahouses.

Arts

Carpets Fit for Kings

Throughout the world, quality Persian carpets fetch exorbitant prices and adorn the grandest hotels and homes. In Iran, however, even the humblest homes have beautiful carpets, many handmade by the women of the households in their leisure time. Carpets are traditionally the only "furniture" in Iranian homes, where the floor is used for sitting, sleeping, and praying. Portable and versatile, carpets are an investment that can be sold in time of need. The most valuable carpets are usually displayed on the walls of a house.

Carpet patterns are often copied from designs drawn on paper. Common motifs include flowers, fruits, and animals, alternating with flowing abstract patterns. Plant dyes produce the rich, wonderful colors. Each region of Iran has distinctive, traditional colors and styles. The finest pile carpets are produced

Below: **Persian carpets are made from mixtures of cotton, wool, and silk. The wool or silk is tied by hand and tightly knotted around a base of cotton or silk threads. A skilled worker can achieve 10,000–14,000 knots a day, and a typical carpet has 14,000– 19,000 knots per square foot (150,000–200,000 knots per square meter)!**

by master weavers in urban workshops. These are often made of silk and can have up to 93,000 fine knots per square foot (1 million knots per square m), producing a painting-like effect. Village and tribal carpets, on the other hand, use coarser materials and have simpler designs. A less expensive alternative to the pile carpet is kelim, a carpet woven like cloth.

Another famous Iranian textile industry is based in the city of Esfahan, where handcut wooden blocks are used to print Iranian designs on cotton fabric. The textile manufacturers normally use natural dyes in shades of brown and red.

Tiny Masterpieces

Iranian artists have been masters of the art of miniature painting since the twelfth century. Painted onto bone or leather using a brush made with a single hair, the images are so tiny that they can only be appreciated through a magnifying glass. Miniature paintings illustrate poems, legends, verses from the Qur'an, and the lives of nobles and royalty. The styles have changed remarkably little over hundreds of years. As apprentices learn the art from masters, they preserve and refine the tradition without changing it.

Handicrafts

Iranian craftspeople produce intricate handicrafts. Weavers, metalsmiths, jewelers, and woodworkers undergo lengthy apprenticeships, making and selling their wares in the bazaars of Iran. Some urban alleyways echo with the sounds of craftspeople hammering pots, samovars, and metal trays into shape. Famous traditional crafts include marketry, the art of assembling intricate picture frames, chess sets, backgammon boards, and other objects from small pieces of wood.

Calligraphy

In Iran, calligraphy, the art of elegant handwriting, reached its peak between the fifteenth and eighteenth centuries. The letters of a calligraphic inscription are written or embellished to resemble an abstract design or a particular object. Inscriptions are usually

PERSEPOLIS

Before the Arab invasion of Iran, early Iranian groups built grand palaces and fortresses, most of which no longer exist today. Although it now stands in ruins, the ancient city of Persepolis is an example of the remarkable architectural achievements of the Achaemenid kings who lived some 2,500 years ago.
(A Closer Look, page 62)

Left: **A metal craftsman shapes a giant copper vessel.**

poems or verses from the Qur'an. Calligraphy is used to decorate almost anything in Iran, from carpets and wall tiles to banners and paintings.

Architecture

It is perhaps in architecture that all the Iranian arts achieve their loveliest expression. Most of the buildings in Iran bear the distinctive influence of Islamic architecture. Mosques and religious schools have domes, minarets, and courtyards. These buildings are often decorated with ceramic tiles, intricate white plasterwork, and colorful mosaics, including mirrored tiles.

Shades of blue are the most common colors in tiled buildings, although intricate, decorated tiles exist in all colors. The most common tile designs include flower, fruit, animal, abstract, and calligraphic motifs.

Left: **The mausoleum of Shah Nematollah Vali, in the town of Mahan in Kerman province, is a superb example of Islamic architecture.**

Music and Dance

Music and dancing are essential parts of any kind of Iranian celebration. Some traditional musical instruments are uniquely Iranian, such as the santir, a type of stringed instrument. Each region in Iran has a distinctive musical style, with regional dances and songs in the local languages. Iranian classical music sets poems to traditional rhythms. Since the revolution of 1978–1979, men and women are not permitted to dance together, and female singers are not allowed to sing for male audiences.

Leisure and Festivals

Iranians are very sociable, and their favorite leisure activities usually involve getting together with friends and family. Other than visiting and talking, only a few leisure activities are available to rural Iranians. Men might visit the local teahouse, whereas women mostly stay at home, enjoying each other's company. Iranians living in the cities can choose from a host of leisure pursuits that change throughout the year, according to the seasons.

Summer Activities

In the summer, most shops and offices close during the hot afternoons, and people sleep after lunch. Once the air cools, city streets come alive with families going for a stroll, window shopping, or stopping to eat ice cream or pastries. Shops stay open until late in the evening, and children can play in the parks until after midnight.

On the fringes of the cities, where the air is fresh, some cafés have tables laid on mountain slopes, on river banks, or over streams of cool water. Most cities organize a municipal fun fair that

TEA AND TEAHOUSES

As the national drink of Iran, tea plays an important part in Iranian social life.
(*A Closer Look, page 68*)

Left: **Iranians living in the city enjoy cycling and relaxing in the park — even when the weather gets a little chilly.**

Left: Iranians relax at a ski resort in the Elburz Mountains.

stays open late into the night during the summer. Many people take their food to the park or any green space, and it is not unusual to see entire families eating a full hot meal by the roadside.

Restaurants and cafés are popular with families and groups of friends, and large cities such as Tehran offer a wide range of cuisine. Nevertheless, many people, especially women, prefer to entertain in the comfort of home because in public, women have to keep their headscarves and coats on, even in summer.

Skiing

Skiing is very popular with the residents of Tehran and other cities located close to the mountains. Peaks in northern Iran remain snowcapped throughout most of the year. Many Tehranis ski every Friday on the slopes overlooking the city. A cable car takes them to the upper slopes quickly, offering spectacular panoramas of Tehran. Women must wear suitable clothing, which often means a long coat and scarf over their ski clothes.

Taking a Break

Tehranis enjoy vacationing in the coastal areas of northern Iran. In the summer, some Iranians vacation in the mountains to escape the city heat. The warm southern coast is a popular winter destination. On public holidays such as New Year, many people travel to historical sites or holy cities for short breaks. On religious holidays, many pilgrims head for cities such as Mashhad and Qom, where saints are buried. Cities such as Esfahan and Shiraz attract sightseers and Iranians who simply want to relax.

Soccer: The National Game

Despite its foreign origins, soccer is the closest thing to a national sport in Iran. All cities have soccer teams, and soccer matches are attended by men of all ages. Women have only recently been allowed to attend soccer matches in major cities. Generally, sporting events and spectators are segregated by gender. Tehran has ten soccer stadiums, one of which seats up to 100,000 fans. Soccer has become a great source of national pride since 1998, when Iran qualified to enter the World Cup championship held in France. Iran defeated the United States in the first round but was knocked out of the competition by Germany.

Above: **Iran's national soccer team played admirably in the 1998 World Cup championship held in France.**

DISABLED ATHLETES

Since the Iran-Iraq War left many young men physically disabled, Iran has been at the forefront in providing opportunities for the disabled, especially in sports. Many Iranians participate in international competitions for disabled athletes.

Other Sports

Wrestling displays are held in the *zurkhaneh* (ZOOR-kha-na), or "house of strength," a traditional kind of gymnasium. Volleyball, table tennis, and the martial arts are popular, with Iran hosting international events in these fields. Both men and women take up shooting. Iranian Linda Farriman represented her country in the shooting event in the 1996 Olympic Games held in Atlanta, Georgia. Iranians also excel at show jumping and other equestrian (horseback riding) events. Member of Parliament Fowzia Rafsanjani is an experienced horsewoman.

Not so Easy for Women

In Iran, all sports for Islamic women must be held in private, women-only stadiums, unless strict Islamic dress codes are observed at all times. Although Tehran has a special sports stadium for Iranian Christians, where men and women can compete together, most women athletes find it a challenge to further their sporting careers in Iran.

THE ZURKHANEH: HOUSE OF STRENGTH

The zurkhaneh — gymnasium, meeting place, and sporting arena combined — brings men together for martial arts and fitness training.
(A Closer Look, page 72)

Below: Iranian women have a fine equestrian tradition.

Secular Festivals

The biggest holiday of the year is *Noruz* (no-ROOZ), the Iranian New Year, which falls on the first day of spring. Celebrated since ancient times, this holiday lasts up to two weeks, during which many shops, offices, and schools are closed.

Another ancient festival is *Shab-e Yalda* (shab-eh yal-DAH), the longest night of the year, when Iranians leave the lights on and stay up all night, eating fruit and snacks.

Many public holidays mark recent historical occasions, such as the 1978–1979 Revolution and the death of Ayatollah Khomeini.

Ramazan and Eid-e Fetr

The ninth month of the Arabic Islamic calendar is *Ramazan* (RAM-a-zahn), or Ramadan, the Muslim month of fasting. During this time, no healthy adult Muslim should eat, drink, or smoke during daylight hours. Restaurants stay open only for foreigners and travelers, who need not fast. The start and end of each day are announced with drums and on radio and television. At mosques, prayer leaders use loudspeakers to announce the sunset prayers, which signify the end of the day's fast.

After a month of fasting, the end of Ramazan is celebrated at the sight of the new moon, and three days of feasting, known as *Eid-e Fetr* (EED-eh FET-reh), follow.

NORUZ: A CELEBRATION OF LIFE

The celebration of Noruz, or the Iranian New Year, is at least three thousand years old and deeply rooted in the traditions of Zoroastrianism, the religion of ancient Persia. Today, the festivities last for thirteen fun-filled days. *(A Closer Look, page 58)*

Left: **Residents of Mahan celebrate the thirteenth day of Noruz at an outdoor concert.**

Eid-e Qorban (EED-eh GHOR-bahn), or the Feast of the Sacrifice, falls about two months after the end of Ramazan, on the tenth day of the Islamic month of Zi-Hajeh, when Muslims make the *hajj*, or pilgrimage, to Mecca in Saudi Arabia. The festival commemorates the faith of Abraham, who, according to the Qur'an and also the Christian Bible, was willing to sacrifice his son to please God. God provided a ram to sacrifice in place of Abraham's son. During Eid-e Qorban, Muslims sacrifice an animal, usually a sheep, and share the meat with the poor in remembrance of Abraham's faith.

Shi'ite Muslim Festivals

Shi'ite Muslims celebrate the birthdays of their saints, such as Imam Ali and Imam Reza. More important for Iranians, however, are the special events that mark sad occasions in their history. The most important month of the year for Shi'ites is Muharram, the month in which the last remaining family members of the Prophet Muhammad were martyred.

Minority Festivals

Iran's religious minorities, such as Zoroastrians, Jews, and Christians, have their own holidays, with government approval. In cities with a sizable Christian population, Easter is often marked with processions.

THE ISLAMIC CALENDAR

Unlike the Western, or Gregorian, calendar, the Islamic calendar is based on the movements of the moon. Therefore, Islamic festivals fall on different dates every year.

ASHURA: REMEMBERING A TRAGEDY

In the year 680, rivalry between Shi'ite and Sunni Muslims reached a terrible climax on the hot and dusty plains of Karbala, in central Iraq. Today, Shi'ite Muslims observe the anniversary of that battle.

(A Closer Look, page 44)

Food

Although some Iranian foods are common to many Middle Eastern countries, Iranian cuisine, as a whole, is unique. Meals typically consist of rice served with heavy meat and vegetable stews, in a combination of sweet and sour flavors. Many Iranian recipes call for huge quantities of green herbs, dried fruits and nuts, and pastes made from pomegranates, dates, or grapes. Popular dishes include meat and fried eggplant with sour grapes in tomato sauce; chicken in ground walnut and pomegranate sauce; meat with spinach and prunes; and meat and black-eyed beans with dried limes in an herb sauce. Soups, omelettes, kebabs (small pieces of grilled meat served on skewers), and rice mixed with meat and vegetables are also widely enjoyed.

Iranian Hospitality

Food is always served on platters, so the diners can choose what dishes they want and in what quantities. Because Iranian hosts like to make their guests feel special, they often serve guests large

YOGURT DELIGHTS

Iranians are very fond of yogurt. A common snack consists of thick yogurt mixed with vegetables or herbs and eaten with fresh bread. Yogurt is also used to make a refreshing drink.

Below: Iranian bread comes in several varieties and is available hot and fresh several times a day from the local bakery, where it is baked in a large clay oven.

Left: **Most Iranians eat on a tablecloth, or *sofreh* (sof-RAY), laid over floor rugs. They sit cross-legged and have individual place settings on the tablecloth. Well-to-do urban Iranians may have large dining tables that seat up to twenty or more guests.**

helpings or pick out choice morsels to pile on their plates. Desserts are not commonly served at home. Instead, most Iranians round off the evening meal with tea, followed by fresh seasonal fruits.

Sweets and Snacks

Iranians love pastries, including baklava (layers of crisp, paper-like pastry, filled with nuts and soaked in sugar syrup). Rice puddings come in a variety of forms, with assorted ingredients — some contain milk, others saffron and rosewater. The most common snack is a selection of dried fruits, nuts, and seeds.

"Hot" and "Cold" Foods

Many Iranians follow a set of food rules that comes from ancient Greek medicine. According to these rules, all foods fall into two categories — "hot" or "cold" — defined not by the physical temperature of the food but by its heating or cooling effect on the individual. The recommended amount of each food varies with the individual's age, sex, temperament, and medical condition. According to this theory, a person who is easily angered should eat "cold," or cooling, foods. Hot and cold foods should be combined with care, especially when the individual is ill. Hot foods include sweets, meats, and eggplant. Cold foods include tea, yogurt, cucumbers, and fish.

CAVIAR: "BLACK PEARLS" OF THE CASPIAN SEA

From the Caspian Sea to the tables of the rich and famous — this is the story of caviar.
(A Closer Look, page 48)

RICE: AN IRANIAN STAPLE

Rice is grown in the coastal provinces of Iran. Usually served as a side dish, it is also the basic ingredient in several popular Iranian dishes.
(A Closer Look, page 66)

A CLOSER LOOK AT IRAN

An illustrious past has made Iranians fiercely proud of their heritage, identity, and beliefs. Besides age-old architectural wonders such as Persepolis and Esfahan, many institutions and practices in Iran today have roots that extend far back into history. Zoroastrianism, a religion that originated in ancient Persia, retains a minority following in present-day Iran. The zurkhaneh still provides an arena for young men to keep fit and practice martial arts and wrestling. The celebration of one of Iran's most festive occasions, Noruz, the Iranian New Year, began as long ago as the sixth century B.C.

Despite revering the legacy of the past, Iranians are conscious of the need for progress. After the ravages of the ten-year Iran-Iraq War, the government is eager to diversify its economy, which has been built largely on the oil industry. Nomadic groups, such as the Bakhtiari and the Qashqai, face pressure to abandon their traditional way of life for permanent settlements and farms or for jobs and homes in the cities. As Iran heads toward a stable future, its people strive to meet the demands of modernization and urbanization, while being faithful to the tenets of their Shi'ite faith.

Opposite: **Boys play in front of a pre-Islamic relief on a stone hill near Tehran. Iran's past survives in its many historical sites.**

Left: **Students at Fazieh Seminary in the city of Qom wear the robes of religious scholars and teachers. The Shi'ite branch of Islam is the dominant force in Iranian politics and culture.**

Ashura: Remembering a Tragedy

When Prophet Muhammad, the leader of the Islamic world, died in A.D. 632, his successor, Abu Bakr, adopted the title *caliph*, meaning "successor," or "deputy." He ruled over an assortment of rival factions held loosely together under the banner of Islam. Gradually, two main factions emerged — the Shi'ites, who believed that Prophet Muhammad's successors had to be descended from him through his son-in-law, Ali, and the Sunnis, who accepted other claims to leadership as well.

Left: **Built in the nineteenth century, the Amir Chakhmaq serves as a stage setting for the traditional Ashura passion play that reenacts the martyrdom of Muhammad's grandson Husayn.**

The Battle of Karbala

In 661, Ali was assassinated, and the caliphate passed into the hands of the Syrian Umayyad dynasty, which had members who were distantly related to Muhammad. However, Husayn, the leader of the Shi'ites, possessed a more direct claim to the caliphate since he was Muhammad's grandson. In 680, supporters of Ali's family, based in the town of Kufah in Iraq, summoned Husayn to the city, promising to make him the caliph of Iraq. Husayn and his entire family set out from Mecca (in Saudi Arabia) toward Kufah, but Umayyad sent soldiers to trap them in the desert, near what is now the holy city of Karbala in Iraq. The soldiers cruelly tortured and killed Husayn and his family members. Not even the women and children were spared.

Below: **Actors perform in an Ashura passion play. More than one thousand years after the death of Husayn, feelings for him are still so powerful that the unlucky actor who plays his killer, Shemr, may be attacked by a distraught audience carried away by the drama.**

Over centuries, the massacre of Husayn's family was immortalized in legend. The anniversary of the killing, Ashura (the tenth day of the Arabic month of Muharram), became a day of public mourning among the Shi'ites. In Iran, the mourning lasts throughout the month of Muharram. Cinemas and concert halls are closed, and black flags are displayed. No one marries or celebrates any event, and, at special meetings, speakers recount the story of Husayn's martyrdom. Neighborhood associations, crafts' guilds, and other organizations spend all year preparing for the activities of Ashura.

The Bazaars of Iran

Bazaar is the Farsi word for "market." However, visitors to Iran may be surprised to discover that the bazaar is more than just a place for shopping — it is the commercial center of each city or town, and the Tehran bazaar is the trading hub of the country!

A typical Iranian bazaar consists of many small shops and businesses within a sheltered, enclosed area. It usually includes a mosque and perhaps even a school, a post office, public baths, banks, and restaurants — like a city within a city. Bazaars have a unique banking system, which operates on the basis of reputation. Unlike in regular banks, bazaar merchants do not need collateral to obtain loans. Many of the shops in large bazaars are bases for major import, export, and manufacturing businesses, with storage facilities all over Iran.

Into a Bazaar

In hot, central Iran, most bazaars are located underground, down a flight of stairs. Entering one is like walking into a vast maze. Beyond the gateway, the paths seem to go on forever. Rays of light

Below: **The Vakil Bazaar in Kerman is renowned for its traditional architecture.**

stream in from the skylights pierced in the high, vaulted ceilings. Along both sides of the narrow paths are the "shops" — some booths, others open-fronted stalls, and still others mere cubbyholes, niches scooped out of the walls. Each shop is filled with wares of some sort: traditional crafts; locally grown spices and dried peas, beans, and lentils; and imported toys, clothes, and kitchenware. In the lanes, genuine buyers push past leisurely browsers. Few things have a fixed price, and a friendly drink of tea is often part of a negotiation. Boys carry trays of tea or plates of rice and kebabs from the restaurants for their employers, the stallholders. Donkeys and motorbikes laden with goods weave their way to the shops in bazaars that are above ground, as no cars can enter the bazaar. Professional porters wait for buyers who require their services. For a fee, they will carry even a refrigerator to a buyer's home.

The bazaar merchants of Iran have strong family, social, and business ties with the country's religious leaders and helped overthrow the monarchy of Iran by withdrawing their political and commercial support. The Tehran bazaar generates over half of all retail and trade activity in Iran and brings in a third of Iran's imported goods.

Caviar: "Black Pearls" of the Caspian Sea

Caviar is the oily roe, or eggs, of the sturgeon fish. Priced at about U.S. $150 per pound (U.S. $330 per kilogram), caviar, nicknamed "black pearls," is one of the most expensive and sought after foods in the world.

Ninety percent of the world's caviar comes from four different types of sturgeon found in the Caspian Sea — *Acipenser guldenstadtii*; *Acipenser ruthenus* (the sterlet); *Acipenser stellatus*;

Left: **Most grades of caviar are grayish, greenish, or black. The rarest caviar comes from the golden eggs of the sterlet. In 1996, Iran exported about 150 tons (136 metric tons) of caviar.**

Left: **Sturgeon are usually caught in huge mesh nets cast from fishing boats. In environmentally friendly operations, female sturgeon are released after their roe are taken. The eggs are cleaned at processing plants, then salted and canned under carefully controlled conditions.**

and *Acipenser huso* (the beluga). At just under 3.3 feet (1 m) in length, the sterlet is the smallest of the Caspian sturgeon, while the largest, the beluga, can reach a length of 24.6 feet (7.5 m), tipping the scales at 2,867 pounds (1,300 kg)! The roe of the beluga, however, are less valuable than those of its smaller sturgeon counterparts.

A Habitat at Risk

In Iran, caviar is such an important product that all aspects of its fishing, production, sale, and export are controlled by the government. A hatchery has been established to try to breed sturgeon commercially, as the caviar industry faces some serious problems. Pollution of the Caspian Sea — from shipping, chemical waste, and oil and gas spills — has drastically reduced the sturgeon population, as have dam projects on the rivers that the fish use for spawning. Sturgeon are protected by law from illegal fishing, but this does not deter poachers tempted by the profitability of caviar. Iran is constantly in dispute with its neighbors over fishing rights, fishing quotas, and caviar smuggling. Due to the dwindling sturgeon population as well as the tightening of fishing laws, the amount of sturgeon fished from the Caspian Sea has fallen from 30,000 tons (27,210 metric tons) in 1985 to just 2,100 tons (1,905 metric tons) in 1994.

Esfahan: Half the World

Located on the Zayandeh River about 210 miles (338 km) south of Tehran, the city of Esfahan has a long and distinguished history extending back to ancient times. First the Arabs and then the Turks made it a capital. In the thirteenth century, Esfahan passed into Mongol hands. It was not until the sixteenth century that the city was reclaimed for Iran by one of the country's greatest rulers, Shah Abbas the Great, who transformed it into a splendid capital. Today, Esfahan is an international heritage site protected by the United Nations Educational, Scientific and Cultural Organization (UNESCO). The city is also Iran's most visited tourist attraction.

Opposite: **One of several lovely bridges built by Shah Abbas, Khaju Bridge is also a dam. The lower level of the bridge contains locks that regulate the river, and the upper bridge bears traffic.**

Architectural Wonders

Shah Abbas spared no effort to adorn his capital with elegant bridges, elaborate mosques, stately religious colleges, and other architectural wonders. Historians and writers have described Esfahan as "half the world" in tribute to the numerous treasures that the city contains — the sights, supposedly, of half the world!

Below: **Esfahan's Ali Qapu Palace was built in the seventeenth century.**

At the heart of Esfahan is the Royal Square, or Image of the World. Measuring about 525 feet (160 m) by 1,640 feet (500 m), it is one of the largest town squares in the world. At one end stands the Royal Mosque, ornamented with five hundred types of intricate blue and gold tiles. At the opposite end of the square lies a huge bazaar, packed with Esfahan's famous craftsmen, plying their trades and wares. The Sublime Door, at which Shah Abbas received foreign dignitaries, adorns the western side of the square. From the balcony of this structure, the shah and his guests would watch royal polo games in the square.

Esfahan Past and Present

During Shah Abbas's lifetime, Esfahan had 162 mosques, 48 colleges, 300 public baths, and 1,802 caravanserais (open courtyards that served as camping grounds for travelers and camel trains). So gracious a host was the shah that entire palaces were devoted to entertaining foreign guests. He moved an entire city of Armenian Christians from Iran's northern border to a new town south of the river from Esfahan, so that the famed Armenian craftsmen could contribute their skills to his capital. Today, Esfahan still supports a large Christian population, with a cathedral and many other churches. A dwindling Jewish population remains from Shah Abbas's tolerant rule.

THE SHAKING MINARETS

Esfahan's tourist attractions include the Shaking Minarets (*below*), two slender towers built over a tomb just outside the city. When a person leans hard on one minaret, the other starts to sway gently — a fascinating architectural quirk!

Getting Married in Iran

An Iranian wedding consists of two parts — the actual wedding ceremony, which usually takes place at home and is attended by close family, and the party or reception, which may take place some time after the ceremony. Many Iranians would not consider a couple truly married until after the reception.

The Ceremony

Although the Muslim requirement for marriage is a simple public agreement and declaration, the Iranian ceremony that accompanies this occasion includes several elaborate and ancient Zoroastrian customs. The bride and groom sit on low stools or perhaps a horse's saddle. A cloth is placed on the floor in front of them. On the cloth are several symbolic items, including lighted candles in an elaborate candelabra with a matching mirror. These are wedding gifts from the groom's family to the bride. There are also eggs to represent fertility; bread and cheese in the hope that the couple will always have food; cookies, sugar candies, and a dish of honey for a sweet married life; and a needle and thread to stitch shut the mouths of interfering in-laws!

GIFTS

Wedding gifts commonly consist of gold coins, jewelry, or money and are announced publicly by an attendant. The bride wears all the gold jewelry. In addition, the groom and his family usually present the bride with an agreed amount of gold as assurance that she will be well provided for in her marriage.

Left: **More and more young Iranians are dating in public before marriage, although religious Iranians still object to men and women socializing in public.**

At the announcement that they are married, the bride and groom feed each other by hand with sweets and honey and admire each other in the mirror. They then sign a lavishly decorated marriage contract, which details all conditions important to the couple. These could include whether the woman can continue her profession, how many children they want, where they should live, or the circumstances under which the woman may ask for a divorce.

The Reception

The wedding reception is held at home or in a hotel or ballroom. A large number of guests represents good luck for the couple. The reception usually includes a sumptuous meal, music, and dancing. After a tour of the neighborhood with headlights glaring and horns blaring to announce the wedding, the bride and groom arrive at the reception in a car decorated with fresh flowers. The bride often wears a Western-style white gown and veil. At the end of the reception, as the bride and groom leave for their honeymoon, they have to evade a trail of honking cars in a noisy chase.

Above: **Throughout the wedding ceremony, women hold a white cloth over the heads of the couple. A happily married woman grinds sugar loaves onto the cloth. The sugar grains are then tipped into the bride's hair. The women chant rhymes and put some stitches into the cloth, which the bride keeps for luck.**

The Iran-Iraq War

Relations between Iran and Iraq have always been difficult. Iraq was once part of the Turkish Ottoman Empire, which waged many wars against the Persian Empire. Today, part of the Iran-Iraq border runs along the Shatt al-Arab, a waterway formed by the joining of Iraq's Tigris and Euphrates rivers. Historically, Iraq jealously guarded the waterway as its only access to the Persian Gulf and a profitable sea trade. In 1975, however, to resolve an Iran-supported Kurdish uprising in Iraq, the Iran-Iraq border was redrawn down the middle of the waterway, dividing it into Iraq- and Iran-controlled banks.

About eighteen months after the 1978–1979 Revolution in Iran, Iraqi leader Saddam Hussein took advantage of the civil unrest and political turmoil in Iran to try and reclaim both banks of the Shatt al-Arab for Iraq. He also wanted to seize the oil-producing province of Khuzestan and prevent Iran's Islamic Revolution from spreading into Iraq.

If Saddam Hussein anticipated an easy victory, he was wrong. Despite the weakened state of their country, Iranians rallied to battle. The war united them against a traditional enemy,

THE IMPOSED WAR

Iranians refer to the Iran-Iraq War as "the Imposed War" because it began with an Iraqi offensive. Iraq, however, maintains that Iran had kept up a series of minor attacks on Iraq for a few months before war broke out.

Below: During the Iran-Iraq War, Iraqi prisoners-of-war were kept in large camps.

Left: People visit the graves of the war dead to weep, pray, and console one another. The fountain at Tehran's largest graveyard, Behesht-e Zahra, flows red on Fridays, in memory of the blood shed by the martyrs. Many houses and offices display black-ribboned photographs of young men killed in the war.

and they saw it as a chance to spread their Islamic Revolution throughout the Middle East. Although Iraq received money and weapons from the West and from other countries around the Persian Gulf, Iran had a bigger army. Many Iranian volunteer troops, including women, children, and the elderly, were prepared to attack in "human waves," believing that if they were killed in battle, they would reach heaven as martyrs.

Other peoples and nations were also caught up in the war. The Kurdish minority in Iraq took advantage of the war and tried to seize part of Iraq for themselves. In 1987, when Iran attacked Kuwaiti oil tankers in the Persian Gulf, the United States and several Western European nations intervened in the war, sending warships to protect the Kuwaiti vessels.

By the time the United Nations brokered a cease-fire in July 1988, Iran and Iraq's economies were in ruins and still the Iran-Iraq border remained unchanged. Military losses on both sides numbered about 750,000 altogether. Many civilians sustained terrible injuries, both physical and psychological, in the war. Almost every Iranian family had experienced the loss of a loved one. In some families, two generations of men were killed.

It was not until 1990 that Iran and Iraq resumed diplomatic relations. Saddam Hussein, then engaged in invading Kuwait, agreed to withdraw Iraqi troops from occupied Iranian territories and divide the Shatt al-Arab waterway between Iran and Iraq. Both countries also agreed to an exchange of prisoners-of-war.

LOOKING BACK AT THE WAR

Today, the Iranian government accords special treatment to disabled war veterans in recognition of their national contributions. Foundations give them financial support, and certain jobs and university places are reserved for them. The families of the veterans or of war dead also have social privileges. In the 1980s, many Iranians felt that the war was a heroic effort against a serious enemy. As the war recedes into the past, however, some young Iranians are beginning to lose their respect for the veterans and to see the war as a tragic mistake.

Nomadic Peoples

The Bakhtiari

No one really knows the origins of the Bakhtiari, although they have been written about since the Safavid era (1501–1722). Legend has it that they migrated to Iran from Syria. Today, they live in the mountainous regions between Chahar Mahall va Bakhtiari, Fars, Khuzestan, and Lorestan, over an area of about 25,000 square miles (64,750 square km). They speak Luri, a language closely related to Farsi and Kurdish.

Bakhtiari nomads live in tents and rely on their cattle for a living. Their migration route from their winter quarters near the warm Persian Gulf to the highlands of the Zagros Mountains is long and dangerous. It takes the Bakhtiari four to six weeks to

Left: A Bakhtiari nomad tends his sheep.

A THREATENED LIFESTYLE

The nomadic lifestyle is slowly disappearing. The development of Khuzestan's oil industry and the resulting urbanization has led to the settling of many Bakhtiari as they take up jobs in the cities. The government does not encourage the wandering lifestyle because nomadic communities are difficult to count and provide with education and health care. Many nomadic groups are gradually settling either in cities or in their winter camps, where they take up farming.

reach their summer pastures, traveling through narrow passes at more than 10,000 feet (3,048 m) in elevation and over distances of up to 150 miles (241 km).

The Bakhtiari are divided into two main clans, the Chahar Lang and the Haft Lang. The tribes were a powerful force in Iranian politics in the nineteenth century. After the 1920s, however, the Iranian government forcibly settled many of the tribespeople, and, by 1979, only 250,000 nomadic tribespeople remained. Estimates of the numbers of Bakhtiari today vary from 450,000 to 800,000, of whom approximately one-third are still nomadic.

The Qashqai

The Qashqai live near the borders of the southwestern province of Fars, an area that has long held strategic and economic importance. They speak a Turkish dialect, and the majority are Shi'ite Muslims. The Qashqai tribal confederation emerged in the eighteenth century, and, by the nineteenth century, they were the best organized and most powerful tribal group in Iran, controlling many non-Qashqai villages and some other tribes. Seeing their autonomy as a threat to its power, the Pahlavi dynasty tried to suppress the Qashqai, and when Khomeini became the ruler of Iran in 1979, he ordered his Revolutionary Guard to break Qashqai power. Today, the Qashqai number about 250,000. They remain fiercely independent and proud, despite government attempts to settle them in permanent homes and occupations and integrate them into mainstream Iranian society.

Below: **Nestled at the foot of the mountains are Qashqai houses made of stone. In recent years, some Qashqai have built semi-permanent villages and adopted a more settled lifestyle than their ancestors.**

Noruz: A Celebration of Life

New Year's Day, or Noruz, is Iran's biggest holiday. It coincides with the spring equinox, a time of year when day and night are of equal length (usually March 20 or 21).

Iranians begin their New Year preparations some weeks before Noruz, with spring-cleaning and the making of new clothes for the family. Lentil or wheat seeds are germinated on a plate, symbolizing the coming of spring. Sweets are prepared, friendships renewed, arguments resolved, and debts settled.

On the Tuesday night before Noruz, people light bonfires and jump over them to purify themselves and keep illness and misfortune away. That week, black-faced clowns known as *Haji Firuz* (ha-jee fee-ROOZ) parade through the streets singing, dancing,

AN ANCIENT CELEBRATION

The earliest known archaeological record of a Noruz celebration dates back more than 2,500 years. Carvings in Persepolis, the capital of the Achaemenid dynasty (559–330 B.C.), depict early New Year celebrations (*left*). Many of the Noruz customs observed in modern Iran go back to the Sasanid dynasty (A.D. 224–651). The Sasanids began their celebrations five days before Noruz. They believed that during this period, guardian angels descended from heaven to visit humans. The angels were welcomed with a spring-cleaning, followed by feasts and festivities. Bonfires were lighted on the rooftops to signal to the angels that everything was ready for their visit.

Left: An Iranian woman prepares the Haft Sinn, a selection of seven symbolic items that begin with the Farsi letter Sinn.

and playing tambourines and kettledrums to usher in the new year. Banks stock up on brand new bank notes for adults to give to children. There is even a radio and television countdown to Noruz.

The Haft Sinn

A few days before Noruz, each household sets up the *Haft Sinn* (haft SEEN), placing on a special cloth a set of seven (haft) items that begin with the Farsi letter Sinn. These items vary from household to household. A typical selection might include sprouts to represent rebirth; an apple for health and beauty; garlic to represent medicine; a wheat pudding to represent transformation (the pudding is plain wheat turned into a sweet substance); vinegar for age and patience; the lotus fruit for love; and sumac berries to represent sunrise, or the triumph of good over evil.

Ushering in the New Year

On Noruz morning, everyone puts on new clothes. The next few days are spent visiting relatives and friends. At each house, children receive gifts of money and candies, toys, or clothes. On the thirteenth and last day of Noruz, it is deemed unlucky to stay indoors, and the parks are crowded with picnicking families.

A LUCKY TRADITION

Goldfish, which are normally very cheap, are suddenly expensive at Noruz, since the Iranians believe that goldfish bring good luck for the new year. Many Iranians keep a goldfish in the house just to display at this time of year!

Oil: "Black Gold"

Oil has played an important part in Iranian life since ancient times. When liquid oil and gas escape to Earth's surface from oil-bearing beds deep underground, these fuels are sometimes ignited by lightning and burst into flames that burn continuously for days or even years. Long ago, people were amazed by this phenomenon because they did not understand it, and they began to worship these fires. When Zoroastrianism became the official religion of Iran during the sixth or fifth century B.C., many temples were built over gas or oil springs to house these "eternal" fires.

A Valuable Commodity

Oil comes out of the ground in a form called crude oil. In the mid-1800s, crude oil began to replace whale oil in lamps and soon was in great demand. With the invention of the automobile and the enhancing of oil refining techniques, oil became indispensable as the chief source of gasoline. Oil extraction became a huge money-making venture, earning oil the nickname of "black gold."

Below: **Sulfur is loaded onto a merchant ship from a petroleum plant jetty on one of Iran's offshore islands.**

Left: Oil is stored in large containers and transported over land and sea in tankers.

Oil was discovered in Masjed Soleyman, in the province of Khuzestan, in 1908. Under the Pahlavi dynasty, it developed into Iran's leading industry. Today, Iran is the world's third largest exporter of oil, and petroleum accounts for more than 80 percent of Iranian exports, providing 40 percent of the government's income. Iran produces about 3.6 million barrels of oil a day, of which 2.5 million barrels are exported.

In an oil refinery, crude oil is heated and left to settle into layers of different oil constituents, such as gasoline, kerosene, paraffin, and bitumen. Iran's large refineries can produce up to one hundred different products from crude oil, including fuel, cosmetics, fabrics, and chemicals.

When It Runs Out . . .

Because oil fields take millions of years to form beneath Earth's surface, the world's supply of oil is limited. Iran has an estimated 90 billion barrels of oil left underground, and this is expected to last until the year 2070, if the oil is extracted at the current rate. Iran is looking for new oil fields that lie beneath the waters of the Persian Gulf, but this is not a permanent solution because those new supplies, too, will be finite. In recent years, the Iranian government has been trying to diversify the economy, so that when its oil fields eventually run dry, other industries will be able to sustain the country.

IF THE PRICE IS RIGHT

Oil prices are a national obsession in Iran, whose economy is dependent on the profits of oil. In recent years, oil prices have been relatively low because the world is oversupplied with oil. The availability of alternative energy sources also means that the demand for oil is slowly falling.

AN ALTERNATIVE SOURCE OF ENERGY

The Iranian government is trying to encourage the use of natural gas instead of petroleum because the country's natural gas reserves are estimated to last until 2200.

Persepolis

When Darius the Great ruled over the Persian Empire from 522 to 486 B.C., he planned a capital city worthy of Jamshid, one of the hero-kings of Persian mythology. The city, Persepolis, came to be known also as the Throne of Jamshid. Set in a plain that was then green and fertile, the ancient city now stands in a desert in the province of Fars.

A Glimpse into the Past

The original Persepolis was a complex of palaces occupying an area of approximately 1,345,500 square feet (125,000 square m). It was surrounded by a wall 13–41 feet (4–12.5 m) high. Darius the Great made the city Persia's capital, replacing Pasargadae, where Cyrus the Great is buried.

Today, Persepolis is a valuable archaeological site that reveals a great deal about the ancient Persians, the peoples they conquered, and their neighboring kingdoms. In particular, the carved stone friezes on the two massive stairways leading to the Apadana, Darius's reception hall, show delegates from the

Below: **About 400 miles (644 km) south of Tehran lie the ruins of the Achaemenid capital of Persepolis.**

nations of the ancient world, each bringing choice gifts and tributes to the Persian king. The carvings depict the fashions and customs of people from as far away as Europe and Ethiopia, as well as the crafts and agricultural products for which their countries were famous.

Other reliefs show the royal lifestyle and the games and hunts that the king and his courtiers enjoyed. Many carvings, such as scenes of Zoroastrian fire worship, relate to religious beliefs or myths. The epic battle between the forces of good (Ahura Mazda) and evil (Ahriman) is also depicted, showing the kings of Iran defeating demons and monsters.

Some carvings from Persepolis have become national symbols of Iran. The *homa* (HOM-ah), a mythical beast that is half horse and half bird, is the symbol of Iran Air, the Iranian national airline. Other fabled creatures featured on the columns and friezes in Persepolis include the two-headed bull and the griffin, a beast with an eagle's head and a lion's body.

In 330 B.C., Alexander the Great conquered Persia, burning Persepolis to the ground. Only a small portion of the city was left, and the capital subsequently declined. Over the centuries, its ruins were swallowed up by the desert. The site was excavated in the 1930s, by an archaeological team commissioned by the University of Chicago.

Qanats: An Ancient Technology

An irrigation technology that began more than two thousand years ago, *qanats* (ghan-AHTS) are underground tunnels that carry water from mountain sources to areas where it is needed for agricultural or domestic use. These tunnels run across distances of up to 50 miles (80 km), reaching a maximum depth of about 98 feet (30 m). In Iran, wells dug in the foothills of mountains collect the seepage from melting snow during the spring thaw. Water from these wells collects in the qanats, which slope downhill to the plains, channeling the water to towns and cities on the central Iranian plateau.

Left: **Qanats can be identified easily — the tunnels have circular air openings, through which dirt is excavated.**

Left: Cracks form in a parched river bed in the Dasht-e-Lut (Lut Desert). In water-scarce central Iran, qanats are a valuable form of irrigation.

Engineering Qanats

Qanats are dug manually and maintained by Iranians whose families have been in this line of work for many generations. Digging and maintaining the deep channels of qanats involve the risk of tunnel collapse, so the ceilings must be periodically shored up and the tunnels cleared of rubbish.

Qanat networks support entire cities in some of Iran's driest regions. As Iran looks into more modern methods of irrigation, however, fewer and fewer qanats have been built in recent years. Today, Iran has about 50,000 functioning qanats.

Respecting the Environment

In the past, qanats were an ingenious and practical way to harness Iran's limited water supply. In farming communities, the water was rationed fairly, and farmers tried to conserve water, especially during the hottest seasons, when even the qanats ran a little drier. Modern irrigation technology, such as the electrically powered water pumps of the 1960s and 1970s, has made larger quantities of water available efficiently and cheaply. However, pumps deplete the stores of underground water more quickly than rain and snow can replace them. As a result, many oases become dry and barren, and entire villages may be forced to move. Among the environmentally conscious, there is now revived interest in qanats, a technology that is perfectly adapted to the environment.

PRIVATE QANATS

Foreign embassies in Tehran are equipped with their own qanats, and well-to-do households have historically occupied the urban areas closest to the source of a qanat, ensuring a plentiful supply of fresh water. Some wealthy households boast of private qanats that feed into the basements of their houses.

Rice: An Iranian Staple

In Iran, rice is served in huge portions, as an accompaniment to almost all main dishes. The rice grown on the wet plains of the Mazandaran and Gilan provinces in northern Iran ranks among the finest in the world. Particularly well regarded is "black-tailed" rice, whose long, thin grains have a small black speck at one end.

Iran's own rice output is insufficient for the country's consumption, so large quantities of rice are imported from India and Pakistan. The long-grained basmati is the most popular variety of imported rice.

Chelo

The Iranians have developed rice-cooking into a refined art. Cooked rice is called *chelo* (CHEL-oh). Chelo needs a considerable preparation time of between four and six hours. It is first soaked in several changes of water and washed free of starch until the water runs clear, then half-boiled in salted water, drained, and dried. Then, the cook prepares a "steaming pan," a heavy pan with a wide base and a thickly padded lid that keeps the steam

Below: **The coastal provinces of northern Iran support thriving rice fields.**

Above: **Chelo (*foreground, left*) is a popular dish at many Iranian dinner parties.**

inside. The cook greases the bottom of the steaming pan with oil or butter and adds a layer of thin bread, sliced potato, or rice mixed with yoghurt and saffron, then places the half-cooked rice on top. Finally, the rice is steamed until fluffy and all the grains are separate. The golden crust at the bottom of the pan is served together with the rice. A little cooked rice mixed with golden saffron is used to decorate the steaming mound of chelo. Sometimes, the dish is served with butter or egg yolk.

Pollo

Pollo (pohl-OH) is half-boiled rice layered and steamed with other, cooked ingredients. Sometimes the ingredients are simple, such as a mixture of meat chunks and lentils or ground meat and beans cooked in a tomato paste. More complex and exotic ingredients include chicken with sour cherries in syrup; cabbage and meatballs cooked in lemon, mint, and saffron; or chicken with pistachios, candied carrots, candied orange peel, almonds, and sour currants, and decorated with sparkling rock sugar.

SAFFRON

Saffron is a brilliant yellow condiment used to color, flavor, and perfume rice dishes. It is made from the yellow stigmas of the pink and violet crocus flower, handpicked during a three-week harvest period in October. It takes 2,000–3,000 crocuses to make one small 0.5-ounce (15-gram) packet of saffron!

Tea and Teahouses

Tea drinking began in China some 5,000 years ago and was brought to the Middle East by traders. Today, some excellent varieties of tea grow in humid northern Iran. Favorite imported varieties, mostly from India and Sri Lanka, include the long-leafed Ceylon and Darjeeling teas.

The Art of Tea Drinking

In Iran, tea is a treasured beverage. It is prepared with ceremony, the preparation and anticipation being part of tea's great appeal.

Iranians drink tea from small glasses with indented waists, set on small china or glass saucers. Tea is also served in small, straight glasses set in decorative metal holders with handles. Samovars (metal urns used for heating water) are usually part of a tea set, which consists also of a teapot, a jug for filling the samovar, and a bowl to catch any drips and to rinse the glasses.

Below: A teahouse owner in Kerman brews the beverage for his customers. Tea is made in a small pot and left to brew over a steaming samovar of hot water. Today, these jars are usually electrically heated, although samovars that are heated by fire, by a cylinder of hot coals, or over a gas ring or fire still exist. The tea in the pot is strong, but each serving is diluted to taste with hot water from the samovar.

Left: **Iranian women relax at a teahouse in Shiraz. Although many now admit women, teahouses were traditionally a male domain.**

In most houses, the samovar is switched on or lighted at dawn and left in use until bedtime.

In order to appreciate the color, clarity, and fragrance of the beverage, Iranians drink tea without milk. Loose sugar is added only in the mornings; most of the time, Iranians drink tea with sugar cubes held in their mouths. The cubes are chiseled off huge loaves of sugar-beet sugar. Tea always comes with bowls of cubed sugar.

A Place for People to Meet

Teahouses are the centers of social life for most Iranians. Inside a teahouse, people may drink tea, eat light snacks, and smoke tobacco through hubble-bubble, or hookah, pipes that can be rented by the hour. (The hubble-bubble is an elongated barrel that contains water. As the smoke bubbles through the water, it is cooled before the smoker inhales it.) In the past, visiting storytellers were a favorite entertainment in village teahouses, as were musicians and singers. Today, however, entertainment usually takes the form of lengthy and animated conversations. The teahouse is also where many business deals take place.

Zoroastrianism

Most early peoples worshiped and feared a pantheon of many gods. They saw gods in nature — in the sun, moon, stars, water, rocks, and caves. Although some gods were considered benevolent, many were believed to possess dreadful powers that they exercised at will. Some of these gods could be appeased only with animal, and perhaps even human, sacrifices.

In the sixth century B.C. or possibly even earlier, Zoroaster, a Persian priest, founded a new religion centered on the idea that all the good forces in the world were united under the authority of one true God, Ahura Mazda, the creator of Earth, the universe, heaven, hell, and all things on or in them. Ahura Mazda battles the dark forces of evil, the devil Ahriman and his demons. Humans may choose to behave well or badly, but if they lead good lives and help goodness prevail in the world, they will be rewarded on the day of judgment, when Ahura Mazda will triumph over Ahriman forever.

Below: Zoroastrian fire temples range from rugged structures carved into mountain slopes to elegant buildings, such as this one in the Yazd province. Zoroastrians revere fire as a symbol of God, of truth, and of God's power to dispel darkness. In some of their temples built over oil or gas springs, fires have been burning continuously for more than two millennia.

By about 500 B.C., Zoroastrianism had spread all over Persia, becoming the official religion of the empire. Its moralistic view of good and evil influenced the Jewish religion, which in turn influenced Christianity and Islam. The Magi, or wise men, who visited Jesus after his birth may have been Zoroastrian priests who had studied the constellations and were seeking a new king foretold in the stars.

A Minority Faith Today

After the Arab invasion of Iran in the eighth century, many Zoroastrian communities converted to Islam. Others moved to India, where they kept their religion despite adopting Hindu clothing and the Gujerati language. Called Parsis, they acquired a reputation for commercial ability and honesty in business. Today, the 100,000 or so Zoroastrians in Iran live mainly in and around the central provinces of Yazd and Kerman and in Tehran. Although they are a minority, Zoroastrianism is recognized as the ancient religion of Iran and has a special place in Iranian society. Symbols of the religion can be found everywhere in Iran, from ancient monuments to modern architecture.

Above: **Until the 1930s, when the Iranian government began to discourage their use, Towers of Silence — huge, open stone structures beyond the city boundaries — marked all Zoroastrian communities. In the towers, dead bodies were left to be eaten by vultures or destroyed by the sun's rays. Zoroastrians believe that this is the only ecologically sound way to dispose of corpses without polluting the environment. Towers of Silence are still used by Zoroastrian communities in Pakistan and India.**

The Zurkhaneh: House of Strength

The zurkhaneh is an ancient Iranian institution whose origins are shrouded in legend. According to some people, the seventh-century Arab invasion of Persia prompted the organization of a secret society dedicated to liberating Persia. Young Persian males joined what became the zurkhaneh, where they practiced martial arts and strenuous physical exercises. Today, the zurkhaneh no longer has a political purpose. It functions as a kind of gymnasium, meeting house, and sporting arena all rolled into one. Almost every Iranian town still has a zurkhaneh in active use.

FROM NOVICE TO PAHLAVAN

A male youth joins a zurkhaneh as a novice and progresses, under the guidance of an expert mentor, through several grades of expertise until he becomes a champion, or *pahlavan* (PAH-lav-ahn). A pahlavan is an honorable person who defends the weak and uses his strength to praise Allah and do good works.

Left: Pahlavan Razaz (*left*) was born in 1863 and died in 1941. Also known as "Pahlavan the Brave," he is considered the greatest master of traditional Iranian martial arts. In this picture, he is posing with one of his students, Pahlavan Mivehchian.

Traditional Exercises

The exercise routine and the clothes of zurkhaneh members are traditionally similar to those of ancient Persian nobles and warriors, as depicted in archaeological carvings and paintings throughout Iran. Today, although modern dress is common, some participants still wear the age-old attire consisting of tight leather breeches without shirts. Zurkhaneh members exercise in a sunken pit surrounded by terraced seats and over-looked by a portrait of Ali, the son-in-law of Prophet Muhammad and a beloved Shi'ite Muslim leader. All zurkhaneh exercise sessions begin and end with a prayer and are devoted to the memory of Ali. Throughout the exercises, an old man chants verses from the *Shahnameh*, an ancient Iranian poem about the exploits of kings and heroes. Drumbeats and a clanging bell mark time. The men whirl heavy Indian clubs, wooden shields, and chains, refinements of ancient Persian weapons. They also do push-ups and lift weights. Wrestlers rub oil all over themselves to slip out of their opponents' clutches. Many zurkhaneh exercises are similar to Far Eastern martial arts and exercise routines in that they are aimed at building strength and stamina and used as an aid to meditation and contemplation.

Above: **Athletes begin their exercises with a prayer in a zurkhaneh in Esfahan.**

RELATIONS WITH NORTH AMERICA

North American missionaries came to Iran during the nineteenth and early twentieth centuries, and U.S. oil companies showed interest in Iran from the 1900s onward. However, significant diplomatic and political ties did not develop between Iran and the United States until World War II (1939–1945). In 1943, U.S. President Franklin Delano Roosevelt met in Tehran with the Russian leader Josef Stalin and Prime Minister Winston Churchill of Great Britain. The three powers agreed to guarantee Iran's independence and to provide postwar economic assistance to Iran. After the war, however, when the Russian presence in the Middle East came to be perceived as a threat to American ideals of democracy and a free market, the United States aided Iran in order to prevent the spread of communism in the Middle East. Since then, Iran's relations with North America have varied enormously, from friendship to hostility to tentative goodwill.

Today, after two decades of isolation dating from the 1978–1979 Revolution, modern Iran is poorly understood in North America, although traditional Persian arts and crafts have always ranked among the world's most esteemed cultural treasures.

Opposite: **An oil rig taps Iran's considerable reserves. Oil prospects drew several North American companies to Iran in the early twentieth century.**

Left: **Soviet leader Josef Stalin (*left*), U.S. President Franklin Roosevelt (*center*), and British prime minister Winston Churchill met at the Tehran Conference held in Iran in 1943.**

The Cold War

Although the democratic United States and the communist Soviet Union were allies during World War II, the incompatibility of their different systems of government became apparent after the war.

Russian troops occupied large areas of Eastern Europe and the Middle East, including Iran, during World War II. The U.S. government was afraid that these territories would become Soviet strongholds. Therefore, when the Soviet Union failed to withdraw its troops from Iran in March 1946 as scheduled, the United States appealed to the United Nations Security Council to warn the Russians to retreat. The Russians withdrew in May 1946.

In the 1950s, mutual distrust gave rise to the Cold War, a period of nonviolent hostility between the two powers. During this time, U.S. interests in Iran were prompted mainly by the desire to prevent the spread of communism in the Middle East.

Economic Interests: Whose Oil?

North American economic interests in Iran began with the development of Iran's oil industry in the early 1900s, when foreign oil companies, such as BP, Shell, and Aramco, began operating in Iran. In the 1950s, Iranian prime minister

Above: **By 1945, Soviet troops had advanced to East Prussia (a region on the Baltic shore of Germany). After World War II, the United States feared Soviet influence in Eastern Europe and the Middle East. This anxiety was a chief motive for American interest in Iran.**

Muhammad Mossadegh decided, with the support of the Iranian parliament and public, to nationalize the oil industry. This meant that all the profits generated by Iran's oil would belong to the Iranian government. Foreign oil companies would lose all their investments in the Iranian oil industry. In protest, Europe and the United States organized an economic blockade that crippled the Iranian economy, leaving the country in chaos.

The economic crisis had led to a new political crisis. Iranians blamed the ruler, Muhammad Reza Shah Pahlavi, for his weak leadership. The shah and his wife fled to Italy, begging the United States to restore order to Iran. In return for U.S. help, foreign oil companies would be permitted to continue controlling much of Iran's oil production.

In 1953, agents from the Central Intelligence Agency (CIA) helped incite a coup that overthrew Mossadegh, who had taken control of the country. The shah was reinstated. Throughout the 1960s and 1970s, Muhammad Reza Shah Pahlavi returned U.S. President Richard Nixon's goodwill with support for U.S. policies. Iran played the role of "Policeman of the Gulf," purchasing all the latest military equipment from the United States.

THE NIXON DOCTRINE

In a 1969 bid to contain communism without committing U.S. troops, U.S. President Richard Nixon announced plans to help pro-Western nations, such as Iran, develop into stable powers by supplying them with American weapons. This resolution became known as the Nixon Doctrine.

Left: **Muhammad Reza Shah Pahlavi of Iran and U.S. President Jimmy Carter exchange smiles in Washington, D.C., on November 15, 1977.**

Revolution and the Hostage Crisis

The shah's social and economic reforms were achieved with the help of North American advisers, but many Iranians felt angry that there was no democracy or freedom of expression in Iran. The 1978–1979 Revolution was partly led by students and intellectuals who wanted democratic reform. With the rise to power of strongly Islamic groups, however, U.S.-Iranian relations suffered. The new Iranian leader, Ayatollah Khomeini, denounced the United States as a "great Satan" and gave his approval when, on November 4, 1979, militant students invaded and seized the U.S. Embassy in Tehran, taking its staff hostage. The United States responded by imposing trade sanctions, deporting Iranian students, freezing Iranian assets, and breaking off diplomatic relations. After a failed mission to rescue the fifty-two hostages, President Carter negotiated for their release. Eventually, on January 20, 1981, after 444 days in captivity, the hostages were released in return for about U.S. $8 billion in frozen Iranian assets.

Left: **Delighted U.S. hostages return from Iran after 444 days in captivity.**

Left: **Lieutenant Colonel Oliver North testified before the Iran Contra committee in Washington, D.C., in July 1987. A Congressional inquiry established that certain members of the U.S. government, including Lieutenant Colonel North and Admiral John Poindexter, the former National Security Adviser, illegally aided rebels in Nicaragua, using funds from the secret sale of weapons to Iran. The Iran Contra Affair greatly damaged U.S. President Ronald Reagan's reputation both in the United States and overseas.**

The Iran Contra Affair

In January 1984, the United States included Iran on its list of nations supporting international terrorism and vigorously pursued a policy of blocking arms supplies to Tehran. In 1985, however, the Reagan administration began secret negotiations with moderate members of the Iranian government. Plans were implemented for the sale of weapons to Iran, in the hope that this would aid in the release of several American hostages being held in Lebanon by Shi'ite terrorists loyal to Iran. In 1985 and 1986, two major arms shipments worth over U.S. $2 billion were halted by U.S. customs officials who did not know that the Reagan administration had authorized the shipments.

At the end of 1986, a Lebanese magazine made public the fact that the United States had been secretly selling weapons to Iran against the publicly stated government policy. The scandal worsened when it was later revealed that part of the profits from the arms sales had been used illegally to fund operations by the Contras, a group of rebels fighting to overthrow Nicaragua's government. The Iran Contra Affair was a major embarrassment to the United States and deeply eroded President Ronald Reagan's power and popularity.

Left: Iranian president Muhammad Khatami talks to the press after meeting with Italian prime minister Massimo D'Alema in Rome on March 10, 1999. Khatami's trip to Italy — the first state visit by an Iranian president to the West since the 1978–1979 Revolution — marked improved relations between Iran and the West.

Current Relations: A New Beginning?

The United States and Iran do not have official diplomatic relations. Until the early 1990s, Iranians still protested against U.S. involvement in the Persian Gulf War and U.S. relations with Israel. Although U.S. president Bill Clinton placed a ban on U.S. trade with Iran in 1995, Persian carpets still arrive in the United States via other countries and are sold mostly by Iranian-owned shops in the United States and Canada. In 1996, the Iran-Libya Sanctions Act was passed, forbidding U.S. companies to do business with companies that invest more than $40 million a year in Iran. The Iranian Trade Association is a U.S.-based group working to end U.S. sanctions on Iran.

Since 1997, however, U.S.-Iranian ties have taken a turn for the better, with Iranian president Muhammad Khatami calling for improved relations. Khatami was recently interviewed on U.S. television by Christiane Amanpour, a British journalist of Iranian and English parentage. Today's Iranian government respects the religious convictions of U.S. Christians, and many Iranians have a great interest in U.S. politics and culture.

RELATIONS WITH CANADA

Government relations between Iran and Canada were established in 1955 and have generally been good. Diplomatic contact was ruptured in 1979 but restored to ambassadorial level in 1990. In 1995, Iran's exports to Canada amounted to $121 million in oil, carpets, handicrafts, and agricultural products, while Canada exported $430 million of goods to Iran, including wheat, corn, and other grains; pulp and paper; industrial and telecommunications equipment; medical and pharmaceutical supplies; and agricultural and livestock technology.

Coming to North America

The first Iranian immigrants arrived in the United States to study in the 1940s, when Iranian universities could not cope with the demand for higher education. Throughout the oil boom years of the 1960s and 1970s, Iranian students formed an established body in North America. They were especially drawn to well-known science centers, such as the Massachusetts Institute of Technology, and warm states, such as California and Texas. Many Iranians trained and worked in the oil and defense industries and in the fields of science, medicine, and engineering. Between 1950 and 1977, the United States received 35,000 Iranian immigrants.

The Islamic Revolution brought a new wave of Iranian immigrants — some 100,000 — to North America between 1978 and 1986. Iranian communities developed in California, Toronto, Vancouver, Chicago, and along the East Coast of the United States, especially in New York City. Los Angeles hosts the largest (300,000) Iranian community in North America and remains the main cultural center for expatriate Iranians. There are about 200,000 Iranians living in Canada.

CAREERS IN NEW HOMELANDS

Many Iranian performing artists were forced to leave Iran after the 1978–1979 Revolution, because the new regime restricted freedom of expression in the arts. Most of these artists moved to North America, where they perform and record for local Iranian-American and Iranian-Canadian communities.

Left: Reza Pahlavi (*right*), son of the late shah of Iran, poses with American designer Yankel Ginzburg in Beverly Hills, California, in 1997.

Iranians in North America

A generation of Iranian-Americans and Iranian-Canadians has been born and raised since the 1978–1979 Revolution. Although most of them have never visited Iran, they speak Farsi and English, socialize with other Iranian families, and take part in Iranian community activities. Many families still have close ties with Iran and receive frequent visitors from their former homeland.

Iranians in North America have their own magazines, newspapers, concerts, cultural organizations, and television and radio programs in areas with large communities. Iranian children usually attend Saturday schools, where they learn Farsi, as well as Iranian poetry, music, and dance. They may also attend special religious instruction classes.

Iranian-Americans are active in most scientific and academic fields. Many also work in the retail and food industries. More than 40 percent of Iranians in North America hold a bachelor's degree or a higher qualification, making Iranian-Americans one of the most highly educated immigrant groups in North America. By voicing their cause in newspapers and working with other interest groups, Iranian-Americans are urging better ties between Iran and the United States.

Left: **American tennis sensation Andre Agassi has Iranian ancestry. He was born and raised in Las Vegas, Nevada. With his 1999 victory in the French Open, he became one of only five players in history to have won all the titles in the Grand Slam (Wimbledon, the U.S. Open, the Australian Open, and the French Open — the tennis circuit's most prestigious tournaments).**

North Americans in Iran

The first Americans to live in Iran were nineteenth- and early twentieth-century missionaries, who went there mostly to minister to the Armenian and Assyrian communities. These missionaries also gained some converts from among the Iranian Muslim population. The missions ran hospitals, clinics, orphanages, and schools, many of which remain today, although they now operate under government control.

After World War II, Iran needed the technical and academic assistance of American experts in many fields and invited technicians and academics to live, teach, and work in Iran. American experts dominated the oil industry, with the help of giant companies, such as Shell and Texaco. American military advisers trained the shah's army in the use of American military equipment and weapons.

During the 1970s, Americans living in Iran at the invitation of the Iranian government were exempt from Iranian laws. This angered Iranians, who felt that they were living in a country overrun by foreigners. After the 1978–1979 Revolution, all American companies were asked to leave and to evacuate their personnel from Iran. Only a small number of Americans lives in Iran today.

Above: **American-style soda accompanies an Iranian picnic lunch.**

Pervasive American Culture

Throughout the Iranian economic boom of the 1960s and 1970s, American culture greatly influenced Iranian society. Despite the hostility that some Iranian groups felt toward American policies and sanctions, many Iranians embraced Western ways of life. Hollywood stars were more famous than Iranian celebrities, and Iranians eagerly followed the American pop music scene and Western fashions. American words such as *disco* became part of Farsi vocabulary, and Iranians bought American cars and furniture. Some buildings in Tehran have American-style architecture.

Iranian Products in North America

Some goods popular in North America originated in Iran. Sugar-based candy was developed by the Persians during the Middle Ages. More recently, Iran introduced North America to innovative techniques of growing and processing pistachios. Iran has also given North America pomegranate molasses, which is used for cooking, and plum paste, which is eaten as a snack.

Soccer

Soccer is Iran's national sport, and the country's participation in the 1998 World Cup was enthusiastically greeted by Iranians and Iranian-Americans alike. In the first stage of the competition, Iran played against the United States. The start of the match provided an opportunity for the Iranian team to demonstrate typical Iranian generosity. Each team member arrived bearing a rose for his opposite U.S. player, and the Iranian captain presented a beaten silver tray and a box of Iranian cookies to the American captain. Such courtesy had rarely been seen at an international soccer match. Iran went on to defeat the United States 2–1, a tremendous victory for a team that had never before experienced a World Cup triumph.

The match was something of a victory for Iranian ethnic pride, too, as North Americans and Iranians discovered a shared passion for soccer. Many Iranian-Americans and Iranian-Canadians supported the Iranian national team publicly, showing a pride and confidence in their ethnic identity that they had not felt in the 1980s, when the hostage crisis evoked strong anti-Iranian sentiment in the United States.

Below: **Spurred on by cheering Iranian supporters, Iran beat the United States 2-1 in the first stage of the 1998 World Cup championship held in France.**

85

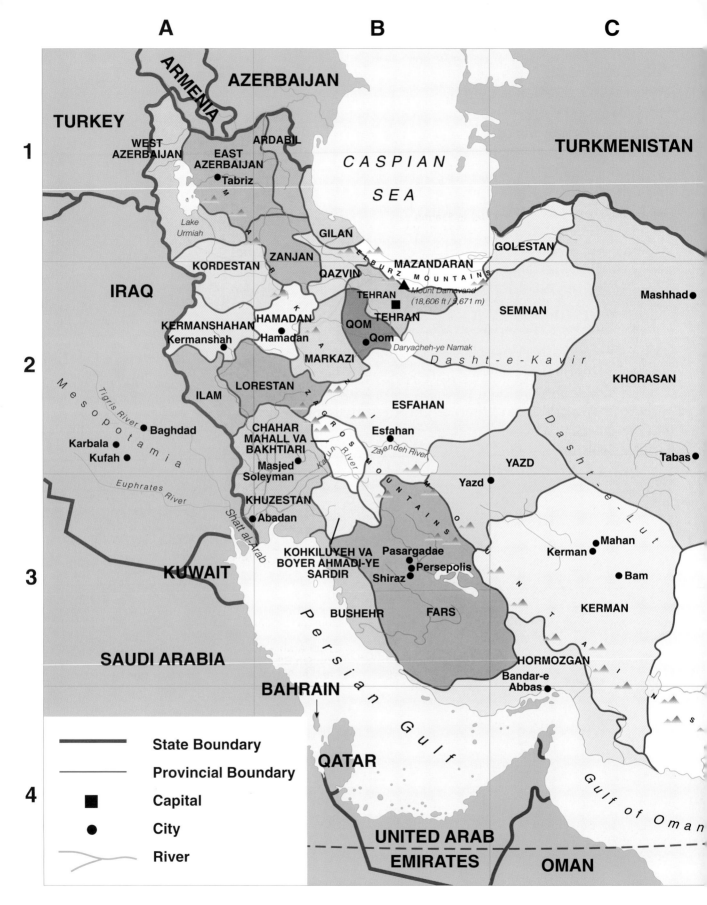

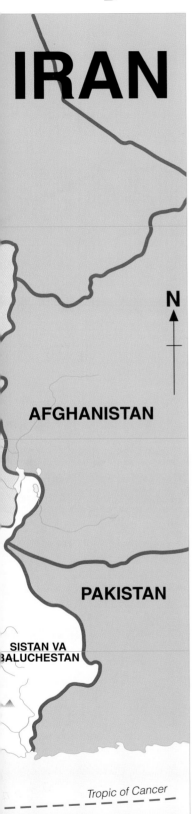

D

IRAN

Abadan A3
Afghanistan D2–D3
Ardabil B1
Armenia A1
Azerbaijan A1–B1

Baghdad (Iraq) A2
Bahrain B4
Bam C3
Bandar-e Abbas C4
Bushehr B3

Caspian Sea B1
Chahar Mahall va
    Bakhtiari B2

Daryacheh-ye
    Namak B2
Dasht-e-Kavir B2–C2
Dasht-e-Lut C2–C3

East Azerbaijan A1–A2
Elburz Mountains
    B1–B2
Esfahan (city) B2
Esfahan (province)
    B2-C2
Euphrates River (Iraq)
    A2–A3

Fars B3–C3

Gilan B1
Golestan C1
Gulf of Oman C4

Hamadan (city) B2
Hamadan (province) B2
Hormozgan C3–C4

Ilam A2
Iraq A1–A3

Karbala (Iraq) A2
Karun River B2–B3
Kerman (city) C3
Kerman (province) C3–
    C4
Kermanshah A2
Kermanshahan A2
Khorasan C1–C3
Khuzestan B2–B3
Kohkiluyeh va Boyer
    Ahmadi-ye Sardir
    B3
Kordestan A1–A2
Kufah (Iraq) A2
Kuwait A3

Lake Urmiah A1
Lorestan A2–B2

Mahan C3
Markazi B2

Markazi Mountains
    A1–C4
Mashhad C2
Masjed Soleyman B2
Mazandaran B2
Mesopotamia (Iraq) A2
Mount Damavand B2

Oman C4

Pakistan D3–D4
Pasargadae B3
Persepolis B3
Persian Gulf B3–B4

Qatar B4
Qazvin B1–B2
Qom (city) B2
Qom (province) B2

Saudi Arabia A3
Semnan B2–C2
Shatt al-Arab A3

Shiraz B3
Sistan va Baluchestan
    C3–D4

Tabas C2
Tabriz A1
Tehran (city) B2
Tehran (province) B2
Tigris River (Iraq) A2–A3
Turkey A1
Turkmenistan C1–D1

United Arab Emirates
    B4–C4

West Azerbaijan A1

Yazd (city) C3
Yazd (province) C2–B3

Zagros Mountains B2–B3
Zanjan B1–B2
Zayandeh River B2

Above: The griffin sculpture is perched on a column in Persepolis. This detail shows one of its two heads.

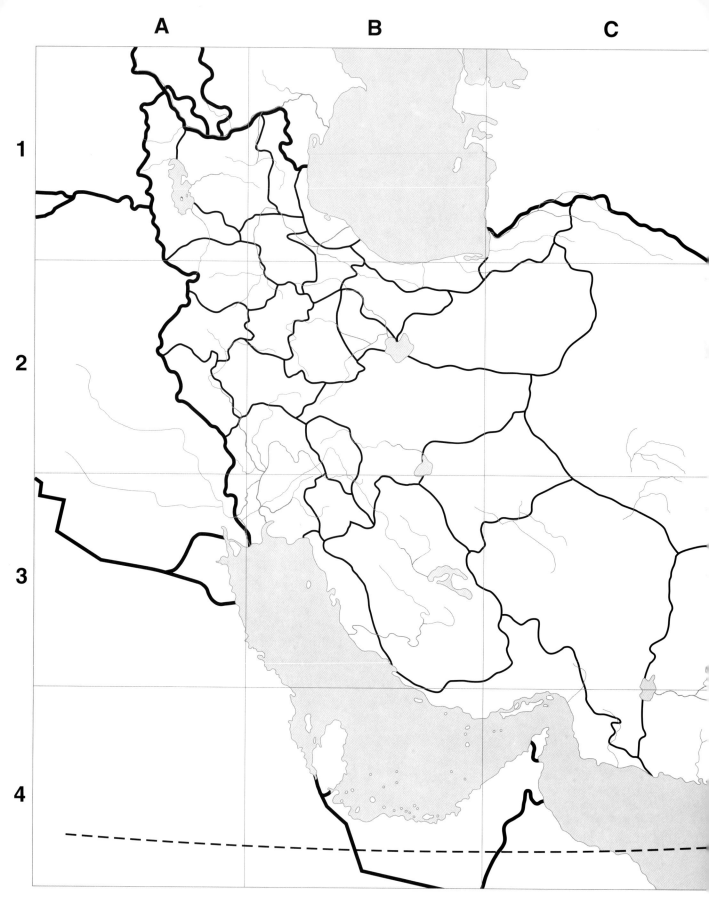

1

2

3

4

D

IRAN

N

Above: **A village sits on hill slopes in the province of Gilan.**

How Is Your Geography?

Learning to identify the main geographical areas and points of a country can be challenging. Although it may seem difficult at first to memorize the locations and spellings of major cities or the names of mountain ranges, rivers, deserts, lakes, and other prominent physical features, the end result of this effort can be very rewarding. Places you previously did not know existed will suddenly come to life when referred to in world news, whether in newspapers, television reports, or other books and reference sources. This knowledge will make you feel a bit closer to the rest of the world, with its fascinating variety of cultures and physical geography.

Used in a classroom setting, the instructor can make duplicates of this map using a copy machine. (PLEASE DO NOT WRITE IN THIS BOOK!) Students can then fill in any requested information on their individual map copies. Used one-on-one, the student can also make copies of the map on a copy machine and use them as a study tool. The student can practice identifying place names and geographical features on his or her own.

Iran at a Glance

Official Name	The Islamic Republic of Iran
Capital	Tehran
Official Language	Persian, or Farsi
Population	68,959,931 (1998 estimate)
Land Area	636,296 square miles (1,648,000 square km)
Provinces	Ardabil, Bushèhr, Chahar Mahall va Bakhtiari, East Azerbaijan, Esfahan, Fars, Gilan, Golestan, Hamadan, Hormozgan, Ilam, Kerman, Kermanshahan, Khorasan, Khuzestan, Kohkiluyeh va Boyer Ahmadi-ye Sardir, Kordestan, Lorestan, Markazi, Mazandaran, Qazvin, Qom, Semnan, Sistan va Baluchestan, Tehran, West Azerbaijan, Yazd, Zanjan
Highest Point	Mount Damavand at 18,606 feet (5,671 m)
Major River	Karun River
Major Mountains	Elburz range, Markazi range, Zagros range
Major Lakes	Caspian Sea, Lake Urmiah
Main Religion	Islam
Ethnic Groups	Persians (51 percent), Azerbaijanis (24 percent), Gilakis and Mazandaranis (8 percent), Kurds (7 percent), Arabs (3 percent), Lurs (2 percent), Baluchis (2 percent), Turkmen (2 percent), others (1 percent)
Major Festivals	Ashura, Eid-e Fetr, Eid-e Qorban, Noruz
National Animal	Persian lion
Exports	Petroleum, carpets, fruits, nuts, animal hides
Imports	Machinery, military supplies, food, pharmaceuticals, metalworks
Major Trade Partners	France, Germany, Italy, Japan, Netherlands, Spain, Turkey, United Kingdom
Currency	Rial (1,741 IRR = U.S. $1 as of 2000)

Opposite: **The famous Gate of All Nations stands in Persepolis.**

Glossary

Farsi Vocabulary

Allah-o-Akhbar (AWL-lah-oo-AKH-bar): God is great.

Ayatollah (EYE-ah-tol-ah): a very learned Shi'ite Muslim clergyman and teacher.

bazaar (bah-ZAHR): a covered market.

chelo (CHEL-oh): cooked, white rice.

Eid-e Fetr (EED-eh FET-reh): the Muslim festival celebrated at the end of Ramazan, the Muslim month of fasting.

Eid-e Qorban (EED-eh GHOR-bahn): the Feast of the Sacrifice, a festival celebrated on the tenth day of the Muslim month of Zi-Hajeh.

faqih (fah-KEEH): the supreme spiritual leader of Iran.

farmandar (far-man-DAR): a town governor.

Haft Sinn (haft SEEN): a special cloth, displayed during Noruz, on which are placed seven items that begin with the Farsi letter Sinn.

Haji Firuz (ha-jee fee-ROOZ): black-faced clowns who parade through the streets during Noruz.

hodood (hoh-DOOD): offences such as adultery, drinking alcohol, and theft, whose punishments are all clearly described in Islamic law.

homa (HOM-ah): a mythical creature that is half horse and half bird.

kadkhoda (kad-KHOD-a): a village headman.

Majlis (MAJ-liss): the Iranian parliament.

mullah (MOOL-ah): a Muslim clergyman or religious expert.

Noruz (no-ROOZ): the Iranian New Year, which falls on the first day of spring.

ostan (oos-TAAN): a province.

ostandar (oos-TAAN-dar): a provincial governor-general.

pahlavan (PAH-lav-ahn): a trained athlete and wrestler.

pollo (pohl-OH): rice cooked with ingredients such as vegetables, fruit, nuts, or meat.

qanats (ghan-AHTS): tunnels that tap underground water sources and channel the water to dry areas.

qessas (gheh-SAAS): crimes, such as murder, that are punishable by retribution.

Ramazan (RAM-a-zahn): the Muslim month of fasting.

Shab-e Yalda (shab-eh yal-DAH): an Iranian festival that celebrates the longest night of the year.

shahr (SHAR): a city.

shahrdar (shar-DAR): a mayor.

sofreh (sof-RAY): a tablecloth laid out on the floor rugs during mealtimes.

zurkhaneh (ZOOR-kha-na): "house of strength"; a traditional Iranian institution that combines the functions of a gymnasium, meeting house, and sporting arena.

English Vocabulary

abdicated: gave up the throne or a similar position of authority.

allocated: set aside for a particular individual, group, or purpose.

breeches: knee-length trousers.

caliphate: a government run by any of the religious and civil rulers of the Islamic world.

collateral: property pledged as security for the repayment of a loan.

condiment: something used to flavor food.

consolidated: united and strengthened.

delectable: delightful, appetizing.

equestrian: relating to horseback riding.

equinox: a time of year when day and night are of equal length.

feudal: relating to an ancient system of government or organization where subjects pledged their service to a lord in return for protection and land.

friezes: panels or parts of walls that are decorated with sculptures and low reliefs.

griffin: a mythical beast with an eagle's head and a lion's body.

hubble-bubble: a pipe with an elongated barrel that contains water.

ibex: a wild mountain goat species.

infrastructure: the fundamental facilities serving a country, city, or area.

irrigation: a means of supplying dry areas with water by diverting streams, building dams and canals, etc.

marketry: the art of assembling intricate objects from small pieces of wood.

martyrdom: the act of suffering or dying for a religious cause.

minarets: tall, often slender, towers attached to mosques.

molasses: a thick syrup produced during the refining of sugar.

municipal: relating to a town or city and its local government.

nationalize: to bring all industries and businesses under government control and ownership.

navigable: deep and wide enough for ships to pass through.

oasis: a fertile area in a desert region.

pantheon: the deities of a particular mythology considered as a group.

pharmaceuticals: drugs and similar medical products.

pygmy: anything very small among its kind.

reliefs: sculptural works that feature subjects raised from the background.

retribution: punishment that is equal to the crime committed.

saffron: a yellow or orange condiment consisting of the dried stigmas of crocuses and used to add color to dishes such as rice.

samovars: metal urns used for heating water.

Shi'ite: Muslims who believe that Ali, the Prophet Muhammad's son-in-law, should have been appointed leader of the Islamic world after Muhammad's death.

stigmas: the flower parts that receive pollen.

succulent: juicy.

succumbed: surrendered; fell.

Sunnis: the majority denomination of Muslims in the world, but not in Iran.

tenets: the principles or doctrines of a particular belief or philosophy.

weaned: accustomed to food other than the mother's milk.

Zoroastrianism: an ancient Persian religion based on the belief that all good forces are united under one God.

More Books to Read

Art of Ancient Iran: Copper & Bronze. Houshang Mahboubian (Philip Wilson)

Ayatollah Khomeini. World Leaders Past and Present series. Matthew Gordon
(Chelsea House)

Iran. Cultures of the World series. Vijeya Rajendra and Gisela T. Kaplan (Benchmark Books)

Iran. Enchantment of the World series. Mary Virginia Fox (Children's Press)

Iran. Major World Nations series. Gary Lyle (Chelsea House)

Iran in Pictures. Visual Geography series. (Lerner)

Iran: Land of the Peacock Throne. Exploring Cultures of the World series. William Spencer
(Benchmark Books)

Kings, Heroes, & Lovers: Pictorial Rugs from the Tribes and Villages of Iran.
Parviz Tanavoli (Interlink)

The Lion and the Gazelle: The Mammals and Birds of Iran. Patrick Humphreys and Esmail
Kahrom (St. Martins Press)

The New Food of Life: A Book of Ancient Persian and Modern Iranian Cooking and Ceremonies.
Najmieh Khalili Batmanglij (Mage)

The Persian Empire. World History series. Don Nardo (Lucent Books)

Videos

444 Days to Freedom: What Really Happened in Iran. (View Video)

Iran and Iraq. (A & E Home Video)

Web Sites

www.salamiran.org/

www.tehran.com/

www-oi.uchicago.edu/OI/MUS/PA/IRAN/PAAI/PAAI.html

www.art-arena.com/iran.htm

Due to the dynamic nature of the Internet, some web sites stay current longer than
others. To find additional web sites, use a reliable search engine with one or more of
the following keywords to help you locate information about Iran. Keywords:
Achaemenid dynasty, Esfahan, Iran-Iraq War, Persepolis, Persian Empire, Shiraz, Tehran.

Index